THANDI

THANDI

Liberation:
My Struggle for South Africa as an Exile in America

Thandeka Luthuli Gcabashe

Elizabeth Enloe and Gloria Gaines, Editors

AFRICA WORLD PRESS

TRENTON | LONDON | CAPE TOWN | NAIROBI | ADDIS ABABA | ASMARA | IBADAN | NEW DELHI

AFRICA WORLD PRESS
541 West Ingham Avenue | Suite B
Trenton, New Jersey 08638

Copyright © 2024 Elizabeth Enloe and Gloria Gaines

All rights reserved. No part of this publication may be reproduced, stored in a retrieval system or transmitted in any form or by any means electronic, mechanical, photocopying, recording or otherwise without the prior written permission of the publisher.

Book design: Dawid Kahts
Cover design: Ashraful Haque
Cover Photo Credit: Permission of Jim Roese

ISBNs: 9781569028216 HB
          9781569028223 PB

Frontispiece collage Photo Credits:
Terry Foss, Permission of AFSC Archives
Permission of Girodano Stolley
Terry Foss, Permission of AFSC Archives
Permission of Gcabashe Family
Terry Foss, Permission of AFSC Archives

Dedication

This book is dedicated to my South African sisters and brothers
For your vision of liberation, courage, and endurance,
For your sacrifices at home and in the wider world
To end apartheid's stranglehold and
Create a nonracial South Africa.

Thank you for your embrace upon my return and
For the opportunity to continue service to our people
As your first ambassador to Venezuela, Columbia,
Ecuador, and the West Indies.

To my friends and colleagues in the United States,
Particularly with the American Friends Service Committee
And the Georgia Coalition for Divestment in South Africa, and
Many others who joined in this long struggle
And made my work possible.

To the memory of Mrs. Coretta Scott King and
Dr. Vincent Harding and Mrs. Rose Harding,
Who sponsored my family in exile.

To the memory of The Reverend Joseph E. Lowery
For his spiritual guidance, and to Mrs. Evelyn G. Lowery for her friendship.

To the memory of my parents,
Nokukhanya Bhengu Luthuli and Albert Mvumbi Luthuli.

To the memory of Phakamele Albert Lincoln Gcabashe, my son.

To my beloved daughters,
Sibongile Gcabashe Montgomery,
Nomhle Gcabashe Canca,
Nokukhanya Gcabashe Warren,
And their families,
And to all my treasured grandchildren and great-grandchildren.

Acknowledgements

There were many challenges in writing this book. My work against apartheid was primarily in the US. When I started writing, I had for many years been back in South Africa and most of the people, records, and documentation that supported my work remained in the US. This circumstance created hurdles that I was able to overcome only through the dedication and hard work of many friends and family.

I am profoundly grateful to those closest to this undertaking who helped bring it to life. Heather Gray assisted with interviews and transcriptions, research, initial drafts, and her extensive knowledge of social justice activism in the South. She was a loyal and able friend throughout this project. Gloria Gaines and Elizabeth Enloe played major roles as editors in bringing the memoir to publication through subsequent research, writing, document and photo retrieval, updating drafts and editing, and sheer tenacity. I knew from working closely with them in Atlanta that they would not give up easily even with the transcontinental obstacles writing the book represented.

Friends and colleagues have honored me with their time reviewing and adding to pre-publication drafts. Dr. Earl Picard contributed substantially to content and review. Carol Luther, David Leonard, Geddes Dowling, Ken Martin, and Jerry Herman provided great feedback that resulted in many rewrites. Lauren E. Moran read and contributed her knowledge of events she documented in her dissertation, *South to Freedom? Anti-Apartheid Activism and Politics in Atlanta, 1976-1990*.

Archivists of the American Friends Service Committee, Donald Davis and Jack Sutters, provided invaluable access and assistance to the AFSC's archival records. Laura McIntyre organized my personal files, classified photos, suggested content designs, and created maps to visualize the work. Sarah Jane McIntyre contributed the black and white images. Andrew McIntyre provided technical support for content sharing.

I am grateful to William Minter who immersed himself into the project with encouraging enthusiasm, suggestions, and resources; and to David Wilk, who provided extensive advice on the art and exacting details of book publishing.

A special thanks belongs to my longtime family friend, Dr. Sibusiso Vil-Nkomo, who invested his friendship, expertise, commitment, and multiple initiatives to advance the project.

I thank my children for their faithful support and comfort throughout the effort, but most especially as my health began to fail toward the latter period. A special thanks to my oldest daughter who remained in the US with her family and provided for my keep on my return trips there, often hosting many of the book's contributors at her home.

Many individuals contributed in a variety of ways—Malkia M'Buzi Moore, Prexy Nesbitt, Richard Knight, Bill Holland, Brian Spears, Sue Ross, Alice Lovelace and others to whom I extend my warmest thanks.

I will forever be grateful to those in my household who for many years have been entrusted with my personal care.

Finally, my thanks are given to Kassahun Checole and Africa World Press for their service in completing what I believe is an important contribution to the history and knowledge of the world's effort to rid itself of the evils of apartheid.

Table of Contents

Dedication	v
Acknowledgments	vii
Table of Contents	ix
Acronyms	xi
Foreword by Sibusiso Vil-Nkomo	xiii
Preface by Gloria Gaines	xv
Introduction	xix

Part I: The Story of My Country: Historical Background

Land and Dispossession of Africans	3
Segregation and Movement of Labor	4
National Party, Racial Classification, Pass System	5
African Resistance, African National Congress	6
ANC Youth League and Defiance Campaign	7
Suppression of Communism Act, Banning, 1956 Treason Trials, General Laws Amendment Act	7
Freedom Charter	8
African Education	8
Sharpeville Massacre	9
Umkhonto we Sizwe (Spear of the Nation), The Rivonia Trial	10
Black Consciousness Movement, Soweto Protests	10
Reserves and Bantustans, Sun City	11
International Outcry and Boycotts	12

Part II: My Early Years

Chapter 1.	Childhood in Groutville	17
Chapter 2.	Early Adulthood in South Africa, 1950s - 1961	31
Chapter 3.	Living on Quicksand: Escape and Exile: 1960s - 1970	39
Chapter 4.	Atlanta, The Early Years: Family, Work, and Activism, 1970 -1981	45

Part III: Liberation Struggle in Exile: My Anti-Apartheid Work

Chapter 5.	Partnerships: My Father and Dr. Martin Luther King, Jr., U.S. Civil Rights Leaders, US Anti-Apartheid Organizations, the United Nations	53

Chapter 6.	Affiliation with the African National Congress, Principles of Kingian Nonviolence	59
Chapter 7.	Beginnings of Anti-Apartheid Work as a Full Time Endeavor, 1981 - 1983	63
Chapter 8.	Apartheid's Ongoing Atrocities	71
Chapter 9.	Education, Education, Education	75
Chapter 10.	Cultural and Sports Boycotts	91
Chapter 11.	Divestment: Federal and State Legislation, Economic Sanctions and Boycotts	99
Chapter 12.	Coca-Cola Divestment Campaign and Coca-Cola Boycott	113

Part IV: After Nelson's Release, 1990 – 1996

Chapter 13.	Nelson's Release and Beyond, Last Years of Apartheid	139
Chapter 14.	Visits Home to South Africa and International Travel	151
Chapter 15.	Returning Home to Vote, the Inauguration of Nelson Mandela, 1994	155
Afterword		159

Annexes

Annex A: Tributes	163
Heather Gray	163
Carol Luther	164
Mack Jones	167
Earl Picard	168
Elizabeth Enloe	170
Annex B: Awards and Recognitions	173

Appendices

Appendix A: Appeal for Action Against Apartheid Joint statement by Chief Albert J. Luthuli and Reverend Dr. Martin Luther King, Jr. December 10, 1962	181
Appendix B: AFSC History with Southern Africa, Highlights	185
Appendix C: Thandi Gcabashe Speaking Engagements	189
Appendix D: Reflections and observations on my visit to South Africa	199
Appendix E: "1994 Elections in South Africa" Presented by Thandi Gcabashe Speech Delivered at the Quaker Meeting House Decatur, Georgia, May 1994	203
Appendix F: Sampling of Newspaper Articles – 1981 - 1994	211

Acronyms

AFSC – American Friends Service Committee
ANC – African National Congress
BCM – Black Consciousness Movement
BOSS – South African Bureau for State Security
GCDSA – Georgia Coalition for Divestment in South Africa
MK – *Umkhonto we Sizwe* ("Spear of the Nation")
NAACP – National Association for the Advancement of Colored People
NP – National Party
PAC – Pan Africanist Congress of Azania/Pan Africanist Congress
SCLC – Southern Christian Leadership Conference

Foreword

By Sibusiso Vil-Nkomo

Thandi Luthuli Gcabashe's writing awakens us to the atrocities of one nation's decades-long endeavor to exclude and oppress the overwhelming majority of its people based on a carefully constructed system of racial classification. During most of the 20th century, the systematic and horrific escalation and brutal implementation of South Africa's apartheid laws denied land, education, livelihood, and citizenship to the country's black, coloured, and Asian people.

Thandi's story, told with her characteristic simplicity and humility, inspires us to recall those amongst us who confront the Goliath of racism on behalf of a multi-racial world. It comes at a time when the world's people reckon anew with historic human rights abuses and with the aspiration for human dignity.

The memoir is largely about Thandi's excellent work in the USA, in particular her Atlanta-based work as a South African exile. Her tireless efforts contributed to the discourse and struggle against apartheid South Africa by progressive Americans. The extent of her commitment and contributions influenced persons of diverse backgrounds and political persuasions, reaching far and wide throughout the USA, with a special resonance among university students.

This is a truthful narration by Mama Thandi. She pulls no punches. The outright opposition and the double dealing of those who did not want to overthrow the apple cart emerge in her narration. These were the true challenges she faced in her own strategic and quiet way as she forged ahead with the struggle to liberate South Africa.

Mama Thandi was a committed liberator while working hard to give her children an outstanding upbringing. I vividly witnessed this when visiting her home in Atlanta. The book is testimony to her as a loving and caring human being.

The strengthening of the divestment movement and the implementation of sanctions by the USA was a major factor in bringing down apartheid. In my thinking, this movement was central to demolishing a system that was declared a crime against humanity. Mama Thandi relates well her role in this regard, and that of progressive Americans and organizations such as the Southern Christian Leadership Conference and the American Friends Service Committee amongst many others she recognizes.

Thandi: Liberation

While Thandi's primary focus is a historic moment in South Africa's history, she leaves us with thoughts of the future. Her life's example will be welcomed in our children's classrooms and homes.

Ultimately, the book is about the ties that bind humankind, during adversity and in good times, and how to sustain the necessary relationships. Thandi's work, as spelled out, demonstrates how we need each other as a human race. She writes not only as a South African but as a citizen of the world.

Sibusiso Vil-Nkomo
Executive Dean, Thabo Mbeki African School of Public and International Affairs, Pretoria, SA
Former Senior Researcher Fellow, University of Pretoria, Centre for the Advancement of Scholarship
Chairperson of Board of Governors, Mapungubwe Institute for Strategic Reflection

Preface

By Gloria Gaines

Tandi's (as we spell it in the US) ability to interact with and command the attention and respect of people across different social, cultural, racial, and economic strata contributed considerably to her success as an exiled freedom fighter. Throughout my association with her and her work with the Southeast Region of the American Friends Service Committee as their Southern Africa Peace Education Program Director, I watched her move with remarkable ease across every societal line you could imagine, from the rich and famous to the anonymous, the poor, the young, and the old. I believe with all my heart that Tandi saw only the humanity, and that of God, in each person she met. She saw only the gifts God gave to every soul He created. That is Tandi's gift. It is a gift she used skillfully to marshal the commitments and connections she needed to successfully create a movement in Atlanta and across the United States and to connect that movement to the international struggle against apartheid.

I met Tandi in October of 1982, at the launch of the Georgia Coalition for Divestment in South Africa. I had recently returned to the United States from two years in Nigeria when that country was actively involved in the struggle for freedom and the decolonization in Southern Africa, particularly Zimbabwe. I had lived almost all my life in Georgia, having been raised in Albany and lived in Atlanta since 1970. As can be imagined, during my early years there was little information and no activity anywhere in Georgia centered on political conditions in that part of the world. I left Atlanta in 1979 for an assignment to prepare master plans for the six oldest Nigerian universities. It was in Nigeria that I gained a reasonable understanding of apartheid and its horrific impact on the people of South Africa. As I made plans to repatriate in late 1981, I was pressed strongly by friends to connect in some meaningful way with the international struggle. I left Nigeria with that promise in 1981.

I did not make good on that promise until I saw an article in *The Atlanta Voice*, a local African American newspaper, asking interested citizens to attend an informational meeting on the subject. I phoned Tandi to get the details and met her at the gathering. Meanwhile, I found what little information was available at the time and was prepared to participate fully in what was, in fact, an organizing meeting for Atlanta. We met in the basement of the First Congregational Church in downtown Atlanta. The crowd was sizable, numbering at least sixty. It was broad in make-up, encompassing not only students but also black and white, young, and old, and professional and working-class people. The group decided to focus on divestment, which was a major call to the international community by the African National Congress. There were already some activities underway by the Atlanta City Council, Georgia Legislative Black Caucus, professors and students at Atlanta University Center, and by some of the civil rights organizations. The group decided to call itself Georgia Coalition for Divestment in South Africa to capture the growing international interest in putting economic pressure on the apartheid government. I was elected Co-Chair along with Dr. Mack Henry Jones, Professor of Political Science at Atlanta University.

The group, guided by Tandi and the strength of the AFSC, embarked on a multi-pronged approach to divestment. We focused our efforts on local and state government pensions, the Atlanta University's pension funds, union pensions, the entertainment and sports industries, the Krugerrand, and companies doing business in South Africa. In 1985 after a series of consultations with local partners, AFSC's national office in Philadelphia, national organizations such as the American Committee on Africa and TransAfrica, and with the ANC, we settled on a targeted campaign and later boycott of Coca-Cola. The justification for the focus on Coca-Cola was that its headquarters was located in Atlanta, it had a prominent, recognizable label throughout the world, and, most importantly, it was a company that stressed social responsibility as a part of its image.

Against this background, Tandi was able to undertake one of the most remarkable organizing efforts in the US against apartheid that I am aware of. With few resources, she was responsible for raising funds, holding together a broad-based, disparate support group, and galvanizing prominent activists and personalities as well as politicians and grassroots organizations to create a nationwide campaign. Tandi recruited many highly trained Black professionals as ardent supporters of her cause. They included my sister, long-time judge, the Honorable Crystal Gaines, Dr. Helene Gayle, current president of Spelman College, and the late Centers for Disease Control and Prevention specialist, Dr. William 'Bill' Jenkins. That is, indeed, what she did. She did it with grace, a strong will, dedication, hard work, selflessness, and self-sacrifice. She did it with a personal magnetism that, to this day, I doubt she understands or even accepts that she possesses. Many of us referred to ourselves as "Tandi's people" because we knew that, if called upon by her, we could not refuse her compelling personality and the irrefutable need. Although members of the all-volunteer group came and went, Tandi's understanding was clear that she had to work with whatever resources, talent, and commitment she could muster. She was a master at organizing the demonstrations and being on the front lines herself. She was a commanding communicator, both in written format and orally. She could sit across the table from elected officials, college professors, businessmen, labor leaders, and grassroots people and successfully get her message across, creating in the process a loyal and committed cadre of followers, including myself. I became not only a committed activist and follower but an inspired friend.

My friendship with Tandi was quite remarkable, in view of our respective backgrounds. I grew up in a relatively small rural American southern town during the fifties and sixties. Albany was a focal point of the Civil Rights Movement, filled with brutal stories and experiences typical of the segregated South during that era. Many in my broader family were involved in the movement. As a young child I met Dr. Martin Luther King, Jr. on at least two occasions, with my parents at mass meetings held by the Albany Movement. I was born on land that my ex-slave great-grandparents had acquired, surrounded by white farmers and landowners.

I saw my father, a man of great pride, suffer the indignities of segregation more times than I care to remember. It left an impression that I believe fueled my interest in and commitment to ending apartheid. My parents, though not formally educated and with little financial resources, lived with dignity, determination, and respect. My mother never worked outside of the home. She was a traditional wife and mother for the times. She and my father thought her status as a wife and mother was more important than the economic value of the kind of work available to her. My dad worked "from can to cain't" in the vernacular of the South. He would be so tired at the end of the day that he could only sleep and repeat the process again the next day. There were eleven children in the family, and my parents were determined to raise decent, respectful, contributing human beings. This background I share with my friend Tandi. By no means, though, did my family achieve the prominence that her family did, but I believe that our shared love of people, a fierce commitment to freedom and justice, and a simple sense of humanity undergirded our work together and our friendship to this day.

Tandi will never know or understand the privilege she gave me, the privilege of watching her persist against such horrendous odds to end apartheid, to raise her family alone and in exile, and to finally return to South Africa and continue to give more—more as a mother and grandmother, more in nation building as Ambassador, and more in helping to solidify her father's legacy. Through her, I met many South African freedom fighters, including Presidents Mandela, Mbeki, Zuma, and Ramaphosa, as well as Archbishop and Mrs. Tutu, Oliver Tambo, Johnny Makhathini, Dr. Sam Gulube, and Minister Sbu Ndebele. The privilege of just knowing her as a unique and remarkable human being, as a person of international stature and respect, is far beyond any expectation I could possibly have had growing up in Southwest Georgia.

Imagine that! Me, an insignificant little black girl from Albany, Georgia forming such a strong bond with someone such as Tandi. She, indeed, was not a respecter of status, but rather, what I hope, an astute judge of "the content of one's character." It is that light in her that led Tandi to successfully prosecute one of the major international responses that helped to ultimately end apartheid.

Gloria Gaines
Editor, *The Albany Southwest Georgian* Newspaper, Albany, GA, USA
Local Elected Official, Board of Commissioners, Dougherty County, GA
Former Vice President and Assistant General Manager, MARTA, Atlanta, GA
Former Co-Chair, Georgia Coalition for Divestment in South Africa, Atlanta, GA

Introduction

I know without question that there was a target on my back based on the warning messages of the African National Congress that the ominous apartheid noose was closing in on my husband and me.

Our decision to leave South Africa in 1970 with our four children was momentous. In retrospect, the decision could very well have saved our lives. I know that I would not have sat on the side lines as opposition grew and the struggle unfolded. Had we remained, I would surely have become immersed in the political strife in which thousands of black South Africans lost their lives.

As a parent, my goal was to shelter my children and deliver them safely to adulthood. I left home to protect my family and keep it intact and safe. I anticipated and sought a normal and ordinary life in exile in our new home in Atlanta, Georgia though without the support of the family structure I had left behind. For a few years this was possible. I expected apartheid to fall in five to ten years, after which I would return home.

This path, however, was disrupted by forces that I could not foresee. While working and raising our children, my presence was discovered by civil rights leaders and educators at the Atlanta University Center. By virtue of my being a South African, I was seen by the community as a resource of authentic information. As the horrors of apartheid and the viciousness of the South African government became more widely known, I was increasingly asked to speak. The number of requests grew even more after the Soweto Massacre in 1976 and began to come in from other parts of the country, particularly from college campuses. This catapulted me into a spotlight I initially resisted. Yet, I need to say how compelling the call was and how completely consumed by the struggle I became, sometimes to the neglect of my health and my family.

The chapters of this memoir tell the story of my country, my coming of age, and my growing into adulthood in apartheid South Africa. They introduce you to my family, particularly my parents, Nokukhanya and Albert Luthuli. To my mind, who I became and the work I embraced within the international anti-apartheid movement were a result of my upbringing and the example set by my parents—by my mother, who was the financial backbone and nurturer of our family of seven children, and by my father, Chief of our Groutville community and later President-General of the African National Congress, as well as a Nobel Peace Prize recipient.

Thandi: Liberation

The following chapters highlight persons who visited our home in Groutville and later in life became renowned anti-apartheid leaders. They detail my decision to escape South Africa and the tension-filled departure of my family into exile in the United States. It was there I overcame my personal trauma as a result of apartheid and dedicated myself to liberating South Africa—ultimately, my life's mission.

I offer reflection on the similarities between the apartheid laws of South Africa and the Jim Crow laws of the United States—similarities to which both the Reverend Dr. Martin Luther King, Jr. and my father drew attention in their joint 1962 *Appeal for Action Against Apartheid*. These bonds of shared experience brought Nelson Mandela to Atlanta during his historic 1990 world tour.

I seek to pay homage to Atlanta's enduring legacy within the Civil Rights Movement and to offer my respect to those organizations and individuals who, from this experience, turned their attention and devotion to the anti-apartheid movement. I further acknowledge activists throughout the United States and internationally who worked to isolate South Africa economically and culturally and force an end to the apartheid system.

The intensification of the apartheid's restrictive laws in 1981 and the violent reaction by the government to their opposition coincided with my full-time appointment as Director for the Atlanta-based Southern Africa Peace Education Program of the American Friends Service Committee, whose status as a Nobel Peace Prize winner, longstanding position against the ravages of apartheid, and early divestment from companies with presence in South Africa, made for a highly beneficial fit.

Herein, you will find details of our nonviolent opposition to apartheid—the educational, cultural, and divestment campaigns, the community organizing, and the highlights of the nine-year national Coca-Cola Divestment Campaign and Boycott of Coca-Cola products, hopefully instructive for the future.

In my mind and heart, I have no doubt that the international pressure of which I was a part contributed in large measure to the South African apartheid regime's coming to the negotiating table, to the ultimate end of atrocities, and to the peaceful settlement of the conflict in South Africa. It helped make possible the return to South Africa in 1994 for thousands of individuals in exile, to vote for the first time. I was one among them, finally able to live again in my homeland after an absence of twenty-six years.

Part I
The Story of My Country

Historical Background

To tell my story, I must first tell the story of my country, at least enough of it to capture the events and experiences that shaped my life. I was born into a world and at a time when the pillars of apartheid were being installed with the intention that they would remain in place forever.

Land and Dispossession of Africans

The issue of land and who controls the land has always been at the center of modern South Africa's story. For the pastoralist Khoikhoi and the San, who were hunter-gatherers, there was more than enough land. Then, first the Dutch and subsequently the British swept them aside, took the land that they had occupied for millennia, and through military conquest pushed the African populations further inland and imposed settler colonialism on what we know as today's South Africa.

Beginning with conquest, the Dutch and British, separately and together passed laws to remove Africans from desirable areas and proceeded to dispossess Africans of their lands, competing for and dividing territory as circumstance dictated. They populated some of those lands with white settlers and exploited the resources of others. Their intrusions and dispossession precipitated conflicts among Africans that included war and loss of life, territorial expansion, political instability, shifting borders, and migrations.

In the Anglo-Boer War (1899–1902), the British and Boer (Afrikaans-speaking French, Dutch, Flemish, German) settler communities went to war even as both groups fought against the Africans. Superior British firepower won the Boer War, but the United Kingdom acknowledged the language and rights of the Afrikaners. The two agreed on their respective territorial ambitions, with Great Britain as the sovereign. They together proceeded to further dispossess the Africans. The indigenous population would soon occupy less than 92,000 square kilometers or a mere 7% of the total land area. The pact was consecrated in 1910 when the British Parliament created the Union of South Africa as a sovereign nation-state without any accommodation for the indigenous populations.

Segregation and Movement of Labor

The new nation did not represent the interests of Africans, or those of the Indian and mixed-race communities. Before the new government was formed, informal segregation was being practiced and efforts were underway to control the movement and labor of non-whites. By 1911, black workers were barred from holding skilled jobs and going on strike. Pass laws were instituted and enforced, requiring Africans and others to show proof that they were authorized to be in the areas where they were being questioned. Interestingly, this practice is akin to the pass system used in the US slave-holding South for when blacks traveled off the owner's property.

The Native Land Act (1913) restricted black land ownership and prescribed the terms under which Africans could be on white-owned land. It also prohibited blacks from sharecropping, leasing, most forms of tenancy, and even serfdom. The goal was to deprive non-whites of any opportunity to occupy land outside of strictly proscribed areas. **The Native Trust and Land Act (1936)** refined the exclusions and prohibitions. Those measures coincided with the push to force Africans to perform low-wage manual labor on farms, in factories, and in the mines, where gold and diamonds and other precious commodities were being extracted. The land that was available to Africans was mainly in reserves that were segregated from white areas, or in townships that were inconveniently located far from urban areas. Hence, most Africans who worked did so as migrants, either commuting long distances daily or, in the case of miners, for months at a time.

Britain relinquished its last bit of power over the country in 1931 and, for a while, a fully sovereign South Africa operated as a coalition government with English and Afrikaans speakers governing together in the United Party. White supremacy did not abate during this period. All the strictures remained in place—pass laws, land alienation, segregation, and state repression.

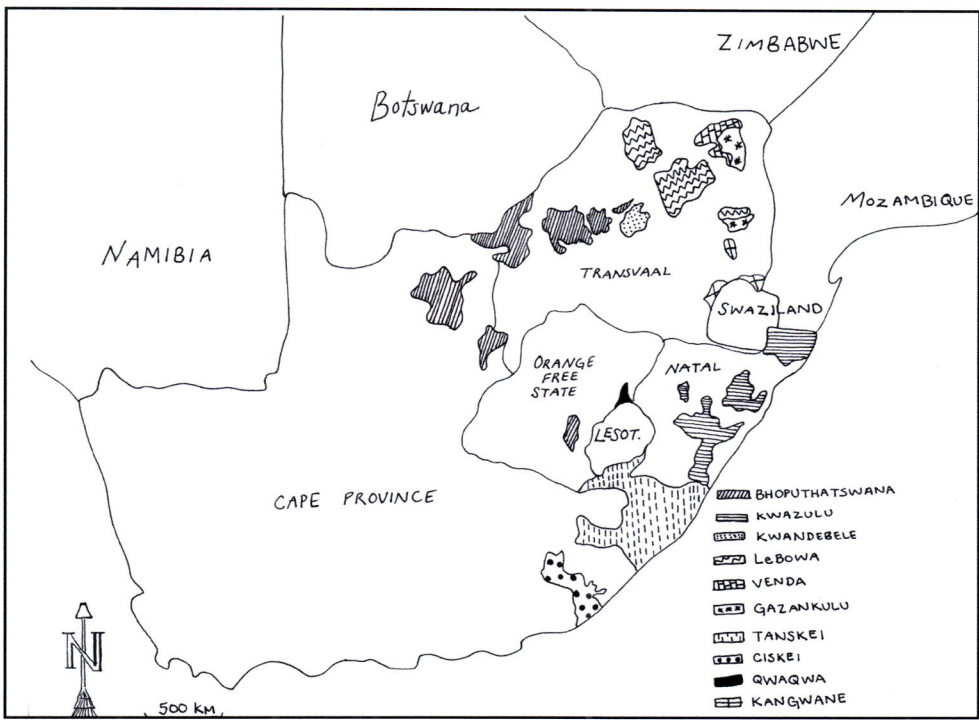

Courtesy of Sarah Jane McIntyre

National Party, Racial Classification, Pass System

The Unity Party split during World War II over support for Nazi Germany. Afrikaner nationalists, vowing to implement a program of extreme institutionalized segregation, formed the National Party (NP) and in 1948 they took power and proceeded to usher in full-blown apartheid. One of their first actions was to enact the **Population Registration Act** (1950), which legalized racial classification and formalized the **Pass System**. The **Extension of University Education Act** (1959) ended the practice of black students attending white universities, mainly the universities of Cape Town and Witwatersrand. Simultaneously, it created separate tertiary institutions for white, Coloured, black, and Asian students.

The first of a series of acts that came to be known collectively as the **Group Areas Act** was passed in 1950. It relegated certain racial groups to specific business and residential sectors in urban areas, thus codifying residential apartheid with mandated African, Indian, and Coloured townships, among other things. It also granted the government the right to forcibly remove Africans from white settlements. It was amended and repealed and reenacted several times before its final repeal in 1991. Also notable is the **Prohibition of Mixed Marriages Act** (1949). That act and the **Immorality Act** (1957) were based on US segregation laws that stood until 1967. The South African law remained on the books until 1985. And all apartheid laws were not eliminated until the new majority government came to power in 1994.

Courtesy of Sarah Jane McIntyre

African Resistance, African National Congress

Africans did not accept those developments without protest. Of course, there were the earlier wars which were lost to superior firepower. But black resistance continued, though initially it was localized and quickly contained by the authorities. Much of the early protest was in the form of polite deputations, petitions, appeals to the authorities and such, but even those protests were ignored or repressed. Those disparate efforts came together on January 8, 1912, when the South African Native National Congress (SANNC) was formed, with a national focus of defending the rights and freedoms of the African population. In 1923 the name of the organization was changed to the African National Congress (ANC). That organization became, and is now, the governing party in a post-apartheid South Africa. It was a long road from those early days of resistance.

The people of South Africa had engaged in a long history of nonviolent struggle. From the time of the founding of the ANC in 1912, the approach of the leaders was to reform the system of colonialism. At its founding, the ANC brought together traditional chiefs, church leaders, representatives from popular organizations, and prominent individuals to focus their efforts and give voice to the African masses. Unfortunately, this was an all-male leadership group. Women only gained affiliate status in 1931 and full membership in 1943. But they went on to develop a powerful women's section and a strong voice in the organization. It was also multi-racial in spirit and fact. Having lived in South Africa, Mahatma Gandhi was an inspiration for many. Indians played an active role in early organizing against apartheid. In 1952 my father was elected President-General of the ANC of which I write more.

ANC Youth League and Defiance Campaign

In 1944 the ANC Youth League was formed, to build nonviolent mass action against the white, minority government. The ANC progressed to a point where its Youth

League pressured the elders to adopt the Program of Action whereby peaceful methods of struggle would be injected with a measure of militancy in disregard of apartheid law. The idea of defying apartheid was firmly established by 1950. There was a stay-at-home strike on May 1, 1950; another stay-at-home strike was called on June 26, 1950 (the first South Africa Freedom Day). This led to the Defiance of Unjust Laws Campaign in 1952.

The campaign was organized by a coalition of protest organizations, including the ANC and the South African Indian Congress, expressly to fight for the political, social, and residential rights of the non-white majority, and to do so countrywide. Up to this point, Africans had been dispossessed of most of the land, were increasingly forced to labor for the settlers, and were being subjected to an evolving system of spatial segregation. The Defiance Campaign called for people to deliberately violate oppressive apartheid laws, using Gandhi's passive resistance strategy. People volunteered to occupy "Europeans Only" public parks, trains, and post offices at the peril of imprisonment. Many trained volunteers registered for the campaign. Some 8,500 people were imprisoned countrywide.

Some gains accrued, e.g., a demonstrable increase in the ANC's membership from 7,000 to 100,000 and removal of the fear of confronting apartheid on the part of ordinary people. These were the first large-scale, multi-racial demonstrations in response to the apartheid regime. It gave rise to the Congress of Democrats, a small but active group of white democrats, and the South African Congress of Trade Unions, which later joined the united front, popularly known as the Congress Alliance. From then onward, resistance was increasingly characterized by demonstrations, mass actions, boycotts, strikes, and a host of acts of civil disobedience. This newfound confidence and attitude among black people, in my opinion, spelled the beginning of the end of apartheid.

At the time, however, those protests were met with repression. The campaign ended in April 1953 after the government passed laws prohibiting protest meetings. Undaunted, in 1957 the ANC called for a stay-at-home strike, which became another passive, disruptive, non-violent tactic in the liberation struggle. In this same period tighter controls were placed on political activities, residency and mobility restrictions became more onerous, and the few non-whites, who had been listed on the electoral rolls, were removed altogether.

Suppression of Communism Act, Banning, 1956 Treason Trials, General Laws Amendment Act

From the beginning, the apartheid government had anticipated opposition and responded to protest initiatives. Immediately following the 1948 election, the National Party had moved to solidify its power with the Suppression of Communism Act (1950), which essentially defined as communist any opposition to apartheid including activities allegedly "promoting disturbances or disorder; promoting industrial, social, political, or economic change in South Africa; and encouraging hostility between whites and nonwhites so as to promote change or revolution."

The ANC, the Pan-Africanist Congress of Azania (PAC), and the South African Communist Party (SACP) were all banned under this law. In what has become known as the 1956 Treason Trial, 156 defendants were detained and tried for high treason. Five years later they were acquitted. In 1963 the government gave itself the power to ban publications to control what was seen and discussed publicly. The 1964 General Laws Amendment Act, known as the Sabotage Act, made sabotage a capital offence and gave the Minister of Justice the power to impose house arrest and detention without trial. In 1982, the Internal Security Act was passed, further criminalizing opposition to apartheid and giving the security authorities tremendous powers.

Banning was a particularly effective weapon in the apartheid arsenal. Banning refers to administrative actions that the apartheid government evolved to use against individuals, organizations, publications, other media, and any entity it deemed a "threat to security and public order." Those actions included restricting a person's movements; determining where they could live and which organizations they could belong to, if any; the forms of communication they were permitted to use; where they were allowed to go; and who they could interact with and under what circumstances. This practice had a real impact on my life and that of our family, as my father was heavily restricted under four separate bans beginning in 1953 until his death.

Freedom Charter

In 1955 a Congress of the People, a multi-racial, multi-organization gathering, adopted the Freedom Charter, which spelled out the aspirations of the African freedom struggle. The Freedom Charter replaced the 1949 ANC Programme of Action (which affirmed an African nationalist perspective) with one that affirmed a multi-racial South Africa. In 1959, differences over those questions and over African nationalism in general resulted in some members leaving the ANC to form the Pan Africanist Congress (PAC). The two organizations became the most prominent and popular political movements against apartheid.

African Education

The School Board Act of 1905 was the first effort to introduce the matter of education for Africans, but it was segregated education from the start. Prior to 1953, only 10% of Africans who received formal education did so outside of mission schools. The mission schools were offshoots of the wide variety of religions that had been transplanted to South Africa since the arrival of the Dutch Reformed Church. They were self-directed from an administrative and educational standpoint, but the government provided essential financial support. Beginning in 1953, the government required the mission schools to formally register with education authorities. It also asserted government control of African education, promptly gearing the curriculum towards an ideological indoctrination to apartheid.

The act created a Bantu Education Department to implement and administer an apartheid policy. While it did set up a separate tribal college system for higher education, it also mandated that those colleges be funded by taxes that only blacks would pay, with absolutely no draw on the national budget. This guaranteed persistent disadvantages in their resources. That Act was followed in 1959 by The Extension of University Education Act, which barred blacks from all-white institutions, which at that time was beside the point because few, if any, blacks were matriculating at white institutions.

A Department of Coloured Affairs was added in 1963, to administer Coloured education, and a Department of Indian Affairs was created in 1965 to control a separate Indian educational system. This was the policy and administrative framework of educational apartheid: create a rigidly segregated educational system designed to institutionalize privilege for the white minority, provide unequal resources, and indoctrinate the non-white population to subordination.

The Sharpeville Massacre

Courtesy of Sarah Jane McIntyre

On March 21, 1960, the Pan Africanist Congress organized a demonstration against the government's pass laws. At what became known as the Sharpeville Massacre, police shot dead 69 demonstrators, including 8 women and 10 children, and injured scores. Many were shot in the back and killed as they fled from the scene. Later that year, because of the massacre, the PAC formed an armed wing, POQO, to fight against the apartheid regime. (The word *poqo* means "pure" or "alone" in South Africa's Xhosa language.) POQO's aim was to destabilize the country, sow mass terror, and foment an uprising. POQO targeted policemen, informers, and traditional leaders who collaborated with the government. They also attacked white civilians, which struck fear among whites and prompted further government repression. During the 1960s, imprisonment and execution of PAC-linked activists accelerated. Those actions devastated POQO, and the organization had difficulty reviving the struggle internally. The organization was laid to rest in 1968 when the PAC launched the Azanian People's Liberation Army in exile.

Umkhonto we Sizwe (Spear of the Nation), The Rivonia Trial

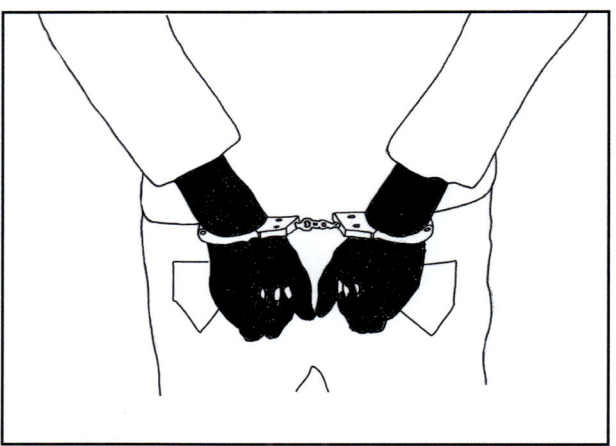

Courtesy of Sarah Jane McIntyre

The ANC leadership also adopted a more militant response. It was after the Sharpeville Massacre that many in the ANC decided they could no longer limit themselves to non-violent protest. Umkhonto we Sizwe (Spear of the Nation, or MK), the armed wing of the ANC, was created in 1961, with Nelson Mandela as its leader. Initially, MK was committed to disabling government facilities and they managed to attack a few. Their modest success was quickly halted by the security state.

The Rivonia Trial (October 1963 – June 1964) delivered a substantial blow to the brain trust of the movement. In total, ten men including Mandela, Walter Sisulu, Govan Mbeki, and Ahmed Kathrada, among others were sentenced to life in prison, most of which was spent on Robben Island. They all served between 22 and 27 years.

Black Consciousness Movement, Soweto Protests

The apartheid government's security regime mounted a more determined opposition campaign that included intense government surveillance and repression. With bannings, detentions, and imprisonment threatening, many black South Africans went into exile. The ANC and PAC formed external resistance organizations to fight the apartheid government. The Black Consciousness Movement (BCM), headed by Steve Biko, also emerged during the 1960s. The BCM sought to assume the mantle of resistance in response to the jailing of ANC and PAC leaders before and following the Sharpeville Massacre. BCM rejected liberal western values and paternalistic attitudes and affirmed an African perspective and mindset. Biko promoted independent black initiative and grassroots self-organization and accepted confrontation with the system as inevitable. He was a key figure in the South African Student Organization, created in 1968, in which Black Consciousness was the official ideology. Biko defined "black" to include Indians and Mixed-Race South Africans. To some extent, Black Consciousness came to influence the opposition generally.

The Soweto protests opposing mandatory Afrikaans instruction and the subsequent massacre—in which 176 people were killed—was inspired by Black Consciousness. The Soweto protests sparked unrest throughout the country.

Reserves and Bantustans, Sun City

No matter how the government approached things, it always came back to land and population. There were too many Africans on lands that the whites coveted and too many more in urban areas than the economy needed. That prompted an effort to permanently remove Africans to certain designated areas. The "native reserves" created out of the Boer War informed the Bantu Authorities Act (1951), which proposed creating African homelands. The Bantu Self Government Act (1959) set up 7 regions called Bantustans, based on the original African Reserves. The list of potential Bantustans was expanded to ten, each a collection of broken and scattered land areas targeted, in most cases, for a specific African population and language group.

With this plan the government intended to define large segments of the population as falling outside the South African state. Blacks would lose their citizenship and voting rights, thus allowing whites to remain dominant in the South African electorate. It was claimed that the Bantustans would eventually move towards self-government. The reality is that they were going to be dependent on South Africa for finance, economic stimulation, and national security. They would have no say in South Africa's affairs, yet they would fall under South Africa's regional security blanket.

Transkei was the first Bantustan to become "independent" in 1976. By 1981, Bophuthatswana, Venda, and Ciskei had followed. The remaining would-be Bantustans were granted a certain measure of autonomy but never completed the four steps required to be declared independent countries by South Africa. No country or international organization recognized the legitimacy of any of the Bantustans. In 1976, in the face of intense South African lobbying, the US House of Representatives took action to oppose recognition.

Courtesy of Sarah Jane McIntyre

The Bantustans were rightfully seen as a convenience for South Africa to rid itself of excess population and avoid financial responsibility for the wellbeing of the displaced. They also became destinations for white South Africans and visitors to partake of casinos, entertainment venues, and interracial gatherings that were banned in South Africa proper. One example is the Sun City casino, hotel, and entertainment complex in Bophuthatswana, which gained international prominence.

Even with the glitter of a place like Sun City and the benefits it brought, mainly in the form of jobs, the Bantustans could not meet the test of independence. Most homelands consisted of scattered segments often bisected by major roads and were shaped to leave untouched areas of importance to South Africa. Together they accounted for only 13% of South Africa's total land area, a portion on which 8 million Africans were expected to live, most of whom were not already there. It was unlikely that many urban dwellers would find those destinations desirable. They were to be encouraged, cajoled, and forced to the homelands. Between 1960 and the 1980s that effort resulted in more than 3.5 million people being forcibly displaced, many of whom ended up in Bantustans.

The forced relocations never substantially changed the population dynamic, since, in the end, only 39% of the black population lived in those areas. As it stood, the homelands had teeming informal settlements, rampant unemployment, withering poverty, migrancy, and family dislocation. The National Party continued to embrace the Bantustan program long after it proved to be a distant dream and it was only fully abandoned in 1994, when the system was dismantled and the territory reincorporated.

International Outcry and Boycotts

The Rivonia Trial, while unsuccessful for the defendants, did generate intense international media coverage and produced great interest in South Africa's status. The "Free Mandela" campaign became a sustained worldwide outcry. In 1958 the ANC initiated an academic boycott of South Africa that drew international attention to South Africa's struggle. More international boycotts were to follow, including a sporting and entertainment boycott. In 1977 Steve Biko, the Black Consciousness leader, who had been banned and was being held under security laws, died in the custody of the South African Security Police. That act galvanized an international outcry. The demand for divestment had gone out as early as the 1960s but it became a real campaign in the 1980s.

It is with divestment and international anti-apartheid campaigns that I come into the picture. That was my life's work. It was how I found a way to contribute.

Part II
My Early Years

1
Childhood in Groutville

Groutville: My Home

I would like to go back now and place myself inside the narrative. I will begin by saying that, despite immense disruptions and indignities, Africans found refuge in family, religion, and community. Such was the case in the small Mission Station of Groutville. It was there I was born on August 13, 1934. Not only was Groutville my birthplace, but it is the ancestral home of my father and what I proudly call my home.

A brief history of Groutville provides a frame of reference for the milieu that shaped my identity. Groutville is located south of Zululand in the Natal Province (KwaZulu-Natal Province, as of 1994), an hour's drive northeast from Durban, the Province's largest city and its hub. The Zulu language is the predominant African language. At home in Groutville we spoke both Zulu and English. The Zulu people are part of the larger Nguni ethnic and language group, and traditionally lived in small communities that farmed and raised cattle. They were made famous in African history by King Shaka Zulu, who is credited with unifying several tribes into the Zulu Nation and expanding Zululand from the early 1800s until his assassination in 1828. Some say that the English propagandists exaggerated his excessive brutality to undermine the Zulus altogether to the advantage of the British colonists. Suffice it to say, as my father noted in his autobiography, Shaka's "occasional ruthlessness was minor by comparison with that of modern dictators, and it was seldom, if ever, as calculated and subhuman as theirs."

British and American Missionaries

The early 1800s was also the era of British and American Christian missionaries and a limited number of conversions to Christianity in our Zululand. Evangelical missionaries from the London Missionary Society began to arrive in southern Africa by 1822. Groutville itself was a creation of American missionaries. The American Board of Commissioners for Foreign Missions, created in 1810 in Massachusetts to deploy missionaries to Africa and elsewhere in the world, sent their first three to South Africa, the Reverends Aldin Grout, Newton Adams, M.D., and George Champion. In December 1835, the Americans arrived at Port Natal and by January of 1836 had traveled to the *kraal* of King Dingane (brother of Shaka), where they reported being greeted "with the utmost kindness and attention." Sometime after this in 1845, Grout settled close to the Umvoti River, where he built the mission station that became today's Groutville.

Charlotte and Alvin Grout

Permission of the Houghton Library, Harvard University

    The name Grout of Groutville was omnipresent in my community, just as Nelson Mandela's name is incorporated today into almost all aspects of South African life. I attended Groutville Primary School. I went to Sunday school and church services at Groutville Congregational Church. And I used to travel to and from the Groutville Train Station to fetch postal letters.

    Symbols and influence of America constantly surrounded me in my early life. Among them were the impressions left by American Board representatives who visited our church and who would occasionally preach at our Sunday service. This was my introduction to the funny American accent with the rolling of the tongue. That was, in fact, the prevailing impression in our community of the American accent—the rolling tongue!

My Parents—Lineage and Marriage

My paternal great grandfather, Ntaba Luthuli, and his wife, Titisi, were among the first Christian converts of Aldin Grout, which makes me the fourth generation in this Luthuli Christian tradition. Ntaba Luthuli became, in 1860, the selected Chief of Groutville, then a burgeoning community. He had two sons, John Luthuli, my grandfather, and Martin Luthuli.

My father, Albert Mvumbi Luthuli, was born about 1898, the younger son of John Luthuli, then an evangelist and interpreter for the Seventh Day Adventist mission, and of Mtonya Luthuli (a child of the royal house of the Zulu King Cetewayo), in Solusi, in what was then Southern Rhodesia, now Zimbabwe. John, his father, died before my father was one year old, leaving my grandmother to raise him and his older brother, Alfred. She sent my father to live in Groutville with her brother-in-law, my father's Uncle Martin, to assure my father had a formal education. Martin Luthuli was, during my father's stay with him, the first elected Chief of Groutville.

Years later, in 1935, when I was but one year old, my father was elected as the fourth Luthuli Chief of Groutville. This chieftaincy position did not follow the Zulu hereditary tradition but, instead it was an elected position and democratically held.

My mother, Nokukhanya Bhengu, was born in 1904 at the Umngeni American Board (Congregationalist) Mission in Natal near Durban. She was the youngest daughter of Maphitha Bhengu, the eldest son of Chief Ndhlokolo of the Ngcolosi clan. He was also a Christian convert and therefore did not inherit the position of chief. He was monogamous, unlike his father, who was polygamous with many wives. Mother lost her own mother early in life and was raised by her sisters at the Umngeni Mission. She attended school at Inanda Seminary and Adams College in Amanzimtoti, just south of Durban, where she became qualified as a teacher.

Both my father and my mother taught at Adams College, an institute of higher learning created in 1853 by the American Board of Missions and named after Newton Adams, one of the original 19th-century American Board missionaries mentioned above. The college has an impressive list of graduates from across the African continent, such as Milton Obote, the former President of Uganda; John Dube, the first President of the African National Congress; Anton Lembede, the first President of the ANC Youth League; Sir Seretse Khama, the former President of Botswana; and, of course, my mother and father.

In 1927, my parents were married and between 1929 and 1945 had seven children. I was the third child of their seven children—four boys and three girls. As a couple, they complemented each other in meaningful ways and endowed me with the values that are deeply embedded in who I am.

Albert and Nokukhanya Luthuli
Permission of Gcabashe Family

Nokukhanya and Albert Luthuli at home
Permission of Gcabashe Family

My Mother—Family Breadwinner, Disciplinarian, and Nurturer

Upon her marriage, my mother gave up her teaching position and became a housewife and mother and also chose to take care of my father's aging mother, who was not well. For most of our growing up years, she was the financial backbone of our family, with earnings coming from her work on the family farm holdings. She was a diligent, hardworking subsistence farmer, plowing and tending to crops that provided our excellent nourishment and our family's sustenance. She was up and gone to the fields before dawn in order to be back home before we went to school.

We raised all our food on the farm. She cultivated everything edible and, thus, my family's grocery list consisted only of items that could not be produced from the soil. To cover those needs, she applied herself to growing sugarcane for commercial trade at a local mill. During the scarcities of World War II, and because of her adventurous spirit, my mother produced soap, candles, toothpaste, and butter at home. It was her business side that made possible the education of seven children.

The mantra of hard work belonged to my mother, and I learned this ethic from her. Often, she would say, "Hard work doesn't kill, it builds a strong character." She inculcated in me the ethos that hard work, with an injection of love and passion, is not laborious but results in a "job well done" and, consequently, perfection is attainable. She drummed into me the virtue of perfectionism that haunts me to this day. Her constant refrain was, "If something is worth doing, do it properly." The problem was that her expectations and standards were so high that we kids

Nokukhanya in her backyard
Permission of Gcabashe Family

thought them unattainable. I still suffer a measure of discomfort if I don't do some things her way.

By profession a teacher, she raised us on "teacher principles," a field that emphasized structure, organization, and thoroughness in whatever task we undertook. My mother taught me that any task, no matter how trivial, required adequate planning to save time and get the best results. My own personal experience with mother's expression of "a job well done" is that it brings pleasure to the eye, mind, and soul.

And she was not stingy on discipline. This was inevitable, given that our father was consumed with public duties of one kind or another and was absent from home most of the time, performing public service as Chief of the Groutville community and later as he became immersed in political activity with the African National Congress.

Despite all the work and discipline, her immense love, tender care, and nurturing of each of us was always apparent. She made me the woman that I am today, minus whatever frailties and shortcomings I might have developed later in life. It is because of my mother's determination and hard work that I say, what I am today is a result of her labor.

The Land and Our Home

Our home was built by my parents on freehold land made possible by the missionaries, who alone, as white people, had the right to purchase and own land. By the incredibly restrictive Native Land Acts of 1913 and 1939, the right to own land was denied to us Africans. Black South Africans had access to only 7%–13.5% of the land in South Africa. The Native Land Acts set the precedent for the brutal apartheid laws of 1948. While we constituted the huge majority of South Africans, we could not own land or be tenant farmers or sharecroppers on white-owned land.

The house itself, by African standards of the day, was structurally and aesthetically acceptable and fit well into our middleclass neighborhood. My mother kept the home intact and provided a viable existence through the thick and thin moments of the struggle against South African oppression. She enhanced its value by her personal landscape design: a hedge around the house, a beautiful lawn, flowers, trees and bushes, an orchard, as well as a vegetable patch. On occasion she had some hired hand to help maintain all of this. As children we enjoyed and were

Luthuli Home in Groutville (2019), currently part of Luthuli Museum
Permission of Elizabeth Enloe

proud of our yard: the exception arrived when we were at an age, determined by our mother, to take on the responsibility of caretaking it ourselves.

Other than festival times, our daily routine was what we thought of as "chaos" because it was filled with chores before we ran off to school. My mother posted a weekly schedule, placing us in pairs of older and younger siblings, to clean the house, cook, do laundry, clean the yard, and fetch water from the river in the dry season or once the tanks were empty. Some of these duties were only for the weekends. Every task was minutely inspected and graded; if it did not meet mother's standard, it was done over and over until she approved. This was so, even if it meant arriving late for school and facing a beating from the teacher.

Weekday evenings also had a routine. After completing our homework and our chores, and playing in the yard with friends, we would wash up and have supper. At our home, we prayed in the morning and in the evening. In fact, our parents conducted evening prayers, which actually turned into mini–church services, with hymn singing, scripture reading, preaching, and prayer. Often, we were given verses to recite the next time. It was quite elaborate.

Sundays were strictly reserved for Sunday school for us children and church services for the adults—except for those of us assigned as the weekend cooks. We attended the Congregational Church that later became the United Church of Christ

(UCC). Religion was central to my family. Sunday lunch was usually luxuriant, with a roast and fitting accompaniments in addition to dessert. There usually was a cake for Sunday afternoon visitors who, for the most part, dropped in unannounced. We children prayed they would not arrive so we could eat the cake. For my mother, Sunday afternoon was the time to concentrate on her correspondence and to pay bills.

A Home for All and Sundry—Learning from My Father

It is customary for Africans to open their homes to the extended family and other travelers or friends. This meant we often had a sizable number of visitors. Given the tendency of youth toward selfishness, we children did not appreciate some features of this practice. It often meant the loss of our precious piece of chicken or our bed. Although we were already a family of nine, in reality, cousins wishing to attend school, and other extended family invariably doubled that number. Relatives who wanted a reliable household and good education for their children found the answer in our home.

I must stress, however, that whatever inconveniences were real or perceived with all of these visitors, they were more than compensated for by family gatherings at Christmas holiday celebrations. On these occasions, we were visited by widowed grandmothers as well as aunties who worked in the vicinity of Durban. Our guests showered us with toys, clothing, and candies. I can never forget the excitement I experienced when receiving my first big doll. It was almost as tall as I was, could stand, and made a sound when it was bent. The Christmas tree, cut from our local area, would be extravagantly decorated. Good food was plentiful. I wished these times could have lasted forever, and it seemed as if the next Christmas took forever to arrive, unlike, at my present age, when the holiday seems to arrive too quickly.

The evenings my father spent at home with us were special. Apart from the prayers, we engaged in a variety of activities. Our father had a passion for music, and with his having been the Choir Master at Adams College, we sometimes sang. We would play Snakes and Ladders, Checkers, a Million Man, and other games. Often, we would sit around the dinner table in endless discussion on basically any issue, but usually on politics. My father was good-natured with all of these discussions, from political to personal issues, such as who we were dating, our friends, sports. You name it, we discussed it. I miss those discussions and I miss him. My sisters and I still talk about that, even today.

Our favorite pastime was debate involving a wide range of topics. I clearly remember the debates on the Defiance Against Unjust Laws Campaign in 1952. Father was alone in believing that nonviolent tactics would succeed in achieving the desired end against the savage laws and the military might of the regime. All of us kids thought the exercise of nonviolence was a waste of time. Of course, now I realize that our father was correct in his views on nonviolence.

I was still a young girl of thirteen in 1948, when my father was invited to speak at the summer camp schools of the American Board in the US. He was away for

Nokukhanya and Albert Luthuli with their children: Sibusiso Edgar, Thandeka Hilda Isabel, Jane Elizabeth Thembekile, Hugh Bunyan Sulenkosi, S'mangele Eleanor, Albertina Nomathuli, and Christian Madunjini

Permission of Gcabashe Family

three months and returned a transformed man in so many ways. He had become accustomed to making his own bed in the morning and he never lost that practice for the rest of his life. He could now prepare his own sandwich, if need be, and he seemed to enjoy the power of choosing and making what items to put in it.

Elementary School—Groutville Primary

I enjoyed school and school sports, but not the corporal punishment permitted at my elementary school. The teachers were allowed to physically punish us if they disapproved of our behavior. I refer primarily to their beating us using a tree branch or a stick. I carry a lifelong emotional scar from one beating by a teacher on my first day of school at Groutville Primary. She asked for my name and when I said "Thandi" she insisted on me having an "English" or "Christian" name. Most of us children had a combination of African as well as English and/or Christian names. It got confusing sometimes.

Thandi, Nokukhanya, and Nomathuli Gcabashe
Permission of Gcabashe Family

But I had no knowledge of my "English" name. I was beaten so severely that I cried and ran home to get my mother who immediately returned with me to settle the matter with the teacher once and for all. Thankfully, she told the teacher that my name was Thandi, that I was registered at the school as Thandi, and there should be no question about this in the future.

This was the epitome of the cultural conflict between African and the European/American cultures, and on my first day of school no less. The teachers were African and, in fact, the teacher who beat me was a friend of my family, who was following orders.

I was an OK student, not particularly exceptional, though notable for solo or lead roles in both school and church choirs. Overall, I remember my childhood with pleasure. It was a time to play until dusk with other children and a time when enduring friendships were forged.

My Father as Chief of Groutville and President of the African National Congress

Our father stopped teaching at Adams College in response to the Groutville community call in 1935 to assume the position of chief. He was much revered in the community.

The chief, now an archaic traditional institution, assisted the king to govern his territory. In the 19th century, chiefs were chosen based on their valor or heroism in war, outstanding leadership, or accumulation of wealth. Because the chiefs lived close to the community, they acted as eyes and ears of the king, in addition to being his advisors and councilors. In the mid–20th century, the era of my father, western colonialism and apartheid had stripped both the kings and the chiefs of the ability to exercise power over their subjects and any semblance of independence was also restricted. Instead, the chiefs often were used as tools and stooges to implement local and national South African government policies. They were supervised by and answerable to a white district magistrate, a great departure from the practice of pre-colonial times.

Father governed over a population of five thousand black African residents of Groutville, officially called the Umvoti Mission Reserve. Part of the population was composed of Christian converts called *Amakholwa*. They were mostly educated and monogamist, with some prone to aspire to so-called civilized western lifestyle. A few exaggerated the style to the extent of being elitist. The majority were called *Amabeshu* and were less likely to be literate. They maintained the traditional ways of polygamy and ancestral forms of spirituality. By law, we were residentially separated from the white community. The only neighboring whites were members of a missionary family, but even they lived quite a few miles from our home.

The duties of a chief involved adjudication over civil disputes, collection of taxes, and granting of homestead sites. A chief was required to have a council to act in an advisory capacity and assist him in the execution of his duties. My father chose the members of his council and we children complained, saying he chose people who were not educated. He then taught us the great lesson that innate intelligence, such as knowing how to manage life and make decisions, has nothing to do with a formal education. While the major or legal disputes would more often go to the magistrate court, what he needed were intelligent individuals who understood the culture and could help "on the ground" to settle the problems of everyday life.

The *Amabeshu* treated my father as a deity or king of sorts, somewhat as was done in pre-colonial times. Some crawled on their knees as a show of respect and recited his praise names in a chant-like fashion from the moment they stepped through the gate of our property. The praise names are a tradition in the Zulu culture to honor certain individuals or clans. *Mashisa* and *Madlanduna* were two of the Luthuli praise names used by the *Amabeshu* for my father. He did not care much for this honor, but he could not stop what the people believed was right to do. To us children, the practice was fascinating. The same group of people treated us in special ways, but our parents played it down.

Baba, as we called our father, traveled extensively, overseeing the state of conditions in the area for which he was responsible, but he always returned home in the evening. This would change.

Growing up, and very early on, I became aware that, although my father was a public figure as a chief, he was also political. He joined the ANC in 1944 having been drawn in through an Indian leader friend in Natal Province which has a substantial Indian presence. A year later in 1945 he was elected to the ANC's Executive Committee of the Natal Provincial Division and subsequently became its President in 1951. In advance of the 1952 Defiance Campaign, my father was summoned to Pretoria where the government officials demanded he denounce the ANC or lose his largely ceremonial, traditional chieftainship. He refused to denounce the organization and was deposed, undaunted, while maintaining the respect of the community. Later that year, on October 16, 1952, he was elected President-General of the national ANC.

Encroaching unjustly upon him, and our family life, were successive bannings by the apartheid government—in 1953; from 1954 to 1956; for a five-year period beginning in 1959; and for another five years beginning in 1964. The bannings restricted my father from participation in public and political gatherings and confined him to the Lower Tugela in the Groutville area. He was required to report frequently to the South African police. However, the bannings did not prevent him from receiving visitors, authoring speeches, writing, attending a two-year trial for treason (of which he was acquitted in 1958), and traveling to Oslo in 1961 to participate in the ceremony where he was awarded the Nobel Peace Prize.

At our home, people were coming in and out constantly. We were like a public household. The guests were almost always Africans, with very few people of other racial groups. Occasionally, Indians would visit, as our home was near Stanger, with its large Indian community, many of whom were friends of my father. Occasionally, white persons visited, such as Alan Paton, author of *Cry, the Beloved Country*, who was a progressive, liberal person living in Durban. There were also dignitaries such as Robert and Ethel Kennedy from the United States in 1966, who arrived by helicopter during the period of one of my father's bannings. It was a world full of surprises.

I noticed that our non-African visitors were often restless and uneasy, and I came to learn that they were prohibited by law from entering black residential areas. To visit, they were required to obtain a special permit, and I believe that almost all my father's friends never sought a permit. It was illegal for them to come to our home, and yet they came. That explained to me why they were so uneasy when in our house, where their presence, if revealed, could result in their being fined or arrested.

You might ask how they could be disclosed to the government. That was possible because there were many informers. Many! The country was teeming with informers. I remember there were always "hangers on" around our home. We knew that they were on a job for the government.

When my father became the President of the ANC, the visitors included all of the national ANC executive committee as well as other ANC members. One of the visitors was Nelson Mandela, to whom I referred at the time as a big brother. He was just one of the bunch, nice and polite and that was it. My father described him as a very bright young man. None of us knew, of course, that he would one day become the President of South Africa.

Visitors also included ANC stalwarts like Walter Sisulu, Govan Mbeki and even Gatsha Buthelezi, when he was in the ANC Youth League. Buthelezi was, in fact, the most frequent visitor at our home, as it lay between his own home and Durban. These political visitors used our house for accommodation as there were no hotels in those days. This was yet another instance when we often lost our beds and slept on the floor.

28   Thandi: Liberation

Ethel and Robert Kennedy arriving by helicopter
Albert Luthuli with Robert Kennedy

Permission of Gcabashe Family

My Schooling Away from Home Begins— Inanda Seminary

The next huge advancement in my life was when, at age fourteen and after completing grade six at Groutville Primary in 1948, I was to leave home to study at the Inanda Seminary north of Durban. It was customary in South Africa to make this transition to a boarding school, and moving out of the home was the rite of passage to adulthood. My mother had attended Inanda and, at this time, my father served on the seminary's Board. The school was a "girls only" American Board Mission middle-to-high-school facility. I had been looking forward to it with excitement. I thought I would be leaving behind all manual work, as well as any severe punishment for infraction of school rules.

But despite all my excitement, I soon discovered that life at Inanda was tough, regimented, and strict. Many girls found the administration and life there intolerable. One of the challenges was another act of forced cultural assimilation. We were not allowed to speak in our indigenous language and were punished if we did so. The punishment mostly required yard work. It was obviously free labor for the school. In my case, I felt grateful for my mother's disciplined home training. I adjusted easily, with the exception of the food and the manual work.

This was the first time in my life to be taught by white teachers, yet no magic bullet came out of this white instruction, as my examination scores remained the same.

My delight was the sports curriculum. I quickly fell in love with tennis, basketball, and croquet. Music, too, was an extracurricular activity I loved and I was occasionally given solo parts.

Two lessons were embedded in me at Inanda that helped shape my future. One was self-denial in service to others, and the other was a quiet confidence that I could achieve anything upon which I set my mind. Inanda reinforced an ethos that my parents had inculcated in me early in life.

The school had a mandatory community program, in which all students were expected to participate. Under supervision of an elder and in small groups, we permeated neighboring communities to teach Bible lessons. Prior to the day trips, we were thoroughly lectured about our topics and made to feel conversant and familiar with Scripture so that we could perform this important task. Yet it was hard work, as we often covered long distances on foot, up to the Umngeni, in the blazing sun.

Upon graduating from Inanda in 1952, my desire was to pursue a career in social work, but my father convinced me otherwise. He argued that jobs for Africans in social work were scant, tenuous, and fraught with uncertainty. This was true even if you were able to secure a social work job in social services to Africans, which, he said, was not a government priority. On the other hand, both teaching and nursing were guaranteed employment professions for African females, if you had excelled in math and sciences in the matriculation exams before leaving high school.

2
Early Adulthood in South Africa, 1950s–1961

The United Nations Declaration of Human Rights and the South African National Party Election, the Cold War and Anti-Communism

The first articulation by the international community of the rights to which all human beings are entitled was immediately following World War II. Largely in response to the Nazi regime's atrocities and human rights abuses, the UN General Assembly adopted the *United Nations Declaration of Human Rights* in Paris on December 10, 1948.

It was tragically ironic that the passage of the *UN Declaration of Human Rights* occurred in the same year that a splinter group in the US established the "Dixiecrat" Party to maintain racial segregation, and the Afrikaner-led National Party won the election in South Africa. The National Party began to implement more draconian and rigidly punitive apartheid policies against black South Africans, all of which were in direct violation of the *UN Declaration of Human Rights*.

On February 9, 1950, US Senator Joseph McCarthy gave an anti-communist speech before the Republican Women's Club in Wheeling, West Virginia that essentially underscored a growing Cold War hysteria in America. Four months afterwards, on June 26, 1950, the South African government passed the Suppression of Communism Act. Intensified Cold War politics in both countries put activists at risk. The mentality led to persecution of persons thought to be communist, to have communist leanings, or to be conveniently vulnerable to accusations by association. You could say this was a ploy to control and diminish the efforts of those who advocated change.

While it is true that the Communist Party did have a presence in South Africa, as was also the case in the United States, the Suppression Act forced those who were officially members of the party and many other activists underground. Activists in both countries who engaged in and espoused collective advocacy or initiated efforts to assist those discriminated against were labeled communists.

It was the beginning of an oppressive period against the liberation movement and ultimately led to life sentences for many of our leaders, such as Nelson Mandela, Walter Sisulu, and Govan Mbeki.

In the United States, the Cold War also had its impact on the African American Civil Rights Movement. The Southern United States had adopted their own system of legalized racial segregation following the end of Reconstruction through the collection of several pieces of legislation that constituted the Jim Crow Laws. Civil Rights leader, Dr. Martin Luther King, Jr., was labeled a communist in posters throughout the southern US because of his leadership of a mass movement for racial equality and his unyielding opposition to racially oppressive laws. Both my father and Dr. King, neither of whom were in the Communist Party, nevertheless were victims of this oppressive Cold War, anti-communist mentality. By 1957 they were in correspondence with one another of which I'll write in a future chapter.

My Early Political Life with ANC Youth, 1956 Pretoria March, and Arrest

I became a part of the ANC Youth League by virtue of my father's ANC engagement at multiple levels. As a young person, I just progressed—blended into the movement—and became active, involved with the hands-on work of the Youth League.

We youth demonstrated and attended rallies, distributed ANC literature, and helped with the ANC's annual conference. It was a lot of work, making the necessary arrangements. Yet, the conference was fun, especially observing the older people conduct the meetings where I learned about parliamentary procedures, which were helpful in my later organizing work.

The highlight for me as a young person, age 22, was going to Pretoria with 20,000 women in August 1956 to protest the extension of the pass laws to women, requiring that they, along with the men, carry the denigrating passbooks.

In Pretoria I joined with thousands of women from other regions of the country. It was the first time that I stepped out of my comfortable niche in Natal Province. I was finally taking my political activity to Pretoria – the seat of government – which we viewed as the source of all our problems, whether it was the pass laws for women and men, the homeland system that was in the making, the Bantu Education Act, the detentions without trial, and on and on.

The Pretoria demonstration put the black women of South Africa on the political map of apartheid opposition. It was out of this event that the famous saying evolved,

"Now you have touched a woman, you have struck a rock." The event was so well documented in films, and subsequently in song and prose, that it became legendary. The feeling of the day was kept alive, and the experience spread from generation to generation, even to those who never experienced Pretoria.

The march failed in the sense that we still had to carry passes. The government did not change course. But the demonstration succeeded in inspiring us to higher levels of struggle than before. Some of us decided just to ignore the pass law. I was arrested several times; I was put into jail because I never carried a passbook with me. Never, ever in South Africa did I carry a pass.

Attending the protest was the activity that I am most proud of in my political life. The energy and community spirit of it all was powerful and inspirational.

I need to recognize that women—women such as Dorothy Nyembe and Bertha Mkhize—who gave me an essential political education during the Pretoria experience, were from the Durban area, and were not highly educated in the formal school system. They were grassroots women, educated politically through personal experiences and actions. Apart from what I learned from my parents, it was these women who crystallized all I had learned by putting words into action. In concrete and very direct ways, they made me the politically informed person I am today. Later on, Lillian Ngoyi, Mama Albertina Sisulu, Helen Joseph, and others shaped my political outlook immeasurably.

Then, there was a most interesting incident when one of my younger brothers visited me in Durban to shop for school supplies before returning to university. When downtown, I went into a store thinking he was still window-shopping. After waiting for him to join me, I stepped outside to find the police had detained him, for not having his pass, and were putting him in a van. Of course, I protested. The person who detained my brother was not wearing a police uniform, so I asked him to produce his identification document. He was, apparently, secret police in civilian clothing, dressed much as a person in domestic service would. It was when he produced his identity, of course, that I realized he was an undercover policeman. He was, in fact, a black African. He was so angry that I had challenged his authority, that he released my brother and apprehended me instead. He also detained me because he demanded my passbook, which I never carried.

I was detained in a holding place unknown to most people. It was not a normal jail or prison. It took days for my husband to locate me so that he could secure my release, pending a formal hearing in court. In fact, the only way he finally found me was through a news reporter who knew about these secret places for holding people. That was quite an experience. It's another long story.

Nursing School—McCord Zulu Hospital, Durban

In 1954, the year my father was banned for the second time, I registered at McCord Zulu Hospital in Durban for a three-year course in nursing. Once again, I was in an American Board Mission facility and learned more about American culture, thanks to the white American hospital doctors.

The superintendent was a tall, large, and older doctor distinguished by a deep baritone voice with the strongest American roll of the tongue I had yet to experience. Younger American doctors joined the hospital staff and their behavior and interaction with senior nursing staff members was radically different. Whereas the older doctors promoted and maintained puritanical ideas and behavior, with lines clearly divided between them and us, the new generation was more relaxed, informal, and interactive with the black staff. They were keen to learn about the local culture and its peoples and, conversely, to inform us about life in America. We were invited for dinner or cocktails in their homes. This was unlike our experience with English manners and practices that always demanded decorum and adherence to prescribed protocols. There were fewer formalities observed on these occasions.

Nursing in Durban—Umkhumbane/Cato Manor

After qualifying as a registered nurse and a midwife, I worked at the McCord Hospital and its clinics in Durban. One clinic was in Chesterville, a black township, and it serviced a slum area named both Umkhumbane, after the nearby creek, or Cato Manor after the first mayor of Durban. It was the worst slum you could imagine.

The slum was a political hot potato in those days and, working with the families, I gained firsthand insight into the people's dreadful living conditions. Often their homes were one-room shacks, fourteen-by-fourteen feet, which housed twelve to fourteen members of one or two families. The children ranged from infants to toddlers to teenagers. They slept side-by-side and were packed like sardines. No electricity was provided and people improvised with candles. They had no indoor plumbing nor sanitation facilities.

During the apartheid era, the South African government zoned the vast majority of urban area exclusively for white residents. Black South Africans were often forcibly removed from their homes if the government decided that the neighborhood was needed for white residents. Black South Africans were prohibited from owning land or homes in the cities. By the early 1950s, black South Africans were assigned to one of eight "homelands" according to their designated group, from Zulu to Xhosa to Tsonga. The "homelands" only made up about 13% of the country's land, even though South Africa's population was nearly three-quarters black. The Reserves could not support the large population that was forced upon them, and black South Africans continued to migrate to cities in a desperate search for jobs, even though it was illegal to do so. Although sprawling townships surrounded every major city in South Africa, the government viewed hundreds of thousands of black South Africans who lived there as temporary visitors to the cities.

It was under these horrific and inhumane conditions that I was summoned, often in the middle of the night, to deliver babies. I would ask the men and older children to leave the room, but the inebriated ones were difficult to deal with. The children in these settlements were exposed to realities they could not process meaningfully in their young minds.

The conflicts within the community were many, primarily a consequence of lack of work opportunities and excessive drinking. Those men with jobs would go off to work and the women stayed at home as there were no jobs for them. Men would waste money, especially on the weekends, when they would drink at a "Municipal" or government beer hall. The women were very much against the government beer establishments. Often, they would go with their sticks and chase their husbands away from the halls.

Side by side, many women created their own African beer halls in their homes for income, a long-held Zulu tradition of making a low-alcohol sorghum beer or *utshwala*, a Zulu name for beer. As Africans were not allowed to purchase alcohol from bottle stores, it was a thriving business until the government ultimately made these halls illegal, creating hostilities for any number of reasons, not the least of which was the government's monopoly of income with its own halls.

In 1958, the government declared Cato Manor a white area and untold numbers of Africans and Indians were uprooted from their homes. The forced evacuation and closure of the African halls meant the loss of the only income for numerous Zulu families.

The women became political activists. I remember, once, in the midst of all the evacuations and destabilization, they organized a demonstration and were arrested. This was in February 1959, in what became known as the *Cato Manor Riots* or *Natal Revolts*. There was a sea of marching women, so impressive while carrying their sticks and singing. It is one of the events I cannot get out of my mind—ever!

Nursing Lecturer

During this same period, McCord Hospital staff would often ask me to substitute teach in the lecture room. Ultimately, the hospital granted me a scholarship to study with three other African nurses at the University of Natal and to become professionally qualified to lecture to nurses. As the first black Africans to obtain this qualification, we four were pioneers and unique. It was not just a matter of our being the first African tutors, there were neither Coloured, or Indian, or other African trained tutors in those days. We four had qualifications more advanced than those of the white teachers at the hospital, most of whom, as missionaries and RNs, had not been professionally trained and were promoted based on the color of their skin. Up until then, in black nursing schools, we were taught by white instructors who were not trained as tutors.

I liked teaching very much, finding it both challenging and rewarding in particular ways, especially in those days with no other African tutors.

The Flat and ANC Youth League

For a brief period while I lectured at McCord, the hospital provided a flat for my accommodation at 86 Beatrice Street in Durban. The apartheid government's Group Areas Act required Africans to live in racially designated areas and prohibited us from residing in predominantly white urban areas. Given this, my place of residence was exceptional.

I knew many members of the ANC Youth League and it did not take long for them to realize how conveniently my flat was located for their meetings. From then on, the flat became a rendezvous for those working in town, as well as for some who attended school at Natal University. They gathered in my flat before disappearing into their various black townships to adhere to the official 9PM curfew. I was never a part of the meetings, except to provide space, mainly because my hospital working hours did not fit the meeting schedules.

Among the comrades coming to my apartment were Johnny Makhathini, who later became the ANC chief representative in New York; Fred Dube, who served prison time on Robben Island, and later worked at the Mazimbu, an ANC school in Tanzania; as well as George Mbele and Thami Mhlambiso. There was also Selborne Maponya, who at one point served as my father's personal secretary.

It did not take long for us to realize that the much-feared Special Branch, a unit of the South African Police, had gained knowledge of our secret meetings. The Special Branch had a vast network of spies and informants who were always seeking information about those who resisted apartheid. When we realized the Special Branch was aware, our meetings ended.

It is important to note that while the apartheid government had its informers, the ANC also had its informants within the apartheid government. That is how we learned of the Special Branch's knowledge of our meetings—from our own ANC informants. On occasion, the same government spies would be double spies. When some of the ANC informants were detained, they would get information to me, stating "Thandi, this is what's happening." You never knew whom to trust.

Most of those who attended the meetings in my flat were detained by the government. Some never got out of detention for years. Some, in fact, received sentences of 10 years on Robben Island.

It should be kept in mind that under the Anti-Communism Act of 1950, one was guilty simply by association. That meant I was vulnerable, as were many activists.

Saint Aidans Hospital

For reasons unrelated to the Special Branch interference, I soon changed jobs to work at Saint Aidans Hospital, a Coloured and Indian hospital in Durban. Again, it was unheard of for an African to teach in such an institution. The hospital's nursing school section was under threat of closure by the National Nursing Council for failure to meet the required standards. I was hired despite the violation of the Separate Amenities Law stipulating that each race live, work, and serve its designated "Population Group." This meant that, by law, I was supposed to be serving only Africans and certainly not Coloured or Indian patients, much less teaching Coloured or Indian staff.

My sole purpose at the Nursing School was to raise the quality of instruction and the pass rate and, indeed, that was soon achieved to the delight of everyone involved. I left after five years, when going into exile out of South Africa.

Life at Saint Aidans exposed the contradictions of apartheid. The hospital staff had tea together—white, Coloured, Indian—and I was the first and only African in this gathering. According to apartheid laws, such racial mixing was not allowed, as there could be no social contact between different racial groups whatsoever.

Everything worked well until the occasional visits of inspectors from the Nursing Council in Pretoria to evaluate the school. We improvised to protect everyone. I would give a full report to a white sister from the ward, who would then report and sign her name on the books. During the visits I had to disappear into thin air. Were Pretoria inspectors to gain the impression that I was in charge of anything at the hospital, they would have deemed it illegal.

At my farewell party, the truth of my work was revealed by Dr. Monty Naicker. While he was a physician in Durban, he was also a stalwart in the liberation struggle and was in the Natal Indian Congress (NIC). He knew my father. In his official speech, he acknowledged my success in turning around the Nursing School and he revealed for the first time how my appointment as an African for such a top job had generated a heated debate among the hospital board hierarchy. While I appreciated the compliments, what disappointed me the most was that because I am African, my competency was called into question.

Falling in Love and Marriage

Here is a ridiculous story of how love can blind and cause a girl in love to make unintelligent, stupid decisions. As I was getting ready to register at Natal University for a diploma to teach nurses, I was offered a scholarship to study in the United States for a Bachelor of Science degree, and I turned it down. I declined the offer because I was in love with the man I ultimately married, and this in spite of his reassurances that he would wait for me. I did not believe him, nor did I want to lose him.

Thulani Gcabashe was an attorney who studied at the University of Fort Hare in the Eastern Cape, and sometimes his advocacy and legal assistance to liberation advocates got him into trouble with the government.

Later in life, my more mature self regretted forgoing this opportunity of study, given that the apartheid government did not allow a bachelor's degree for black nurses. The nursing diploma was the highest qualification one could attain and, as mentioned above, my group of four black ladies studying at the University of Natal were the first in the country to obtain the diploma.

In 1961 I married Thulani Gcabashe in Groutville, and in line with the insane apartheid laws, whites were barred from attending our wedding.

38 Thandi: Liberation

Thandi with Nokukhanya Luthuli

Permission of Gcabashe Family

Thandi with Albert Luthuli

Permission of Gcabashe Family

Thulani and Thandi Gcabashe, 1961

Permission of Gcabashe Family

We purchased a private home in the Clermont Township near Durban. While Thulani practiced law and I worked as a tutor at St. Aidans, it was the beginning of our family of four children who were named Sibongile Eleanor, Nomhle Jacqueline, Nokukhanya Coretta, and Phakamele Albert Lincoln.

3

Living on Quicksand:
Escape and Exile, 1960s - 1970

Deciding to Leave South Africa

In 1960 the ANC was banned by the government, as were virtually all other anti-apartheid political organizations. It meant the ANC began to build a more intensive underground network.

That same year my father was awarded the Nobel Peace Prize, which he received in 1961 when at last granted permission by the South African government to travel with our mother to Oslo for the award ceremony.

In the 1960s Thulani had been living "under the radar" of the infamous government intelligence service, the South African Bureau for State Security, otherwise known as the BOSS. He had been serving a five-year banning order that was about to expire. Thulani's transgression, we discovered, was a reference by Winnie Mandela, Nelson Mandela's wife, to Thulani and my connection to representatives of Umkhonto we Sizwe, the armed wing of the ANC. These representatives, or cadres as we called them, had penetrated the South African border carrying foreign currency and wanted us to assist them in obtaining a bank money exchange. Thulani had met with the cadres and verified their assertions, but he had declined to offer assistance.

Simultaneously, I had become a marked person or "person of interest" to BOSS, which previously had seemingly ignored my name in the case of ANC Youth League meetings at my flat. Supposedly, I was spared for not having participated in the meetings. But with the recurrent surfacing of my name, information became available to me from reliable ANC sources that my detention was inevitable.

Because of Thulani's ban, the visit from the cadres, and the fact that Thulani regularly defended political detainees in his law practice, he consulted with my father who strongly recommended that he leave the country before the imposition of another ban. There was general speculation that his penalty would be more severe the next time around.

These are the circumstances that led to our choice of going into self-exile. It was a matter of preempting the inevitable in the belief that we could serve a greater good outside the country than in detention or jail.

It was common knowledge that, after the regime declared the ANC illegal, the new reality presented only three choices to political activists: to surreptitiously leave the country; to go into prison (which was considered a waste of human resource if it could be avoided); or to work in the underground network in advancing the work of the movement for as long as it was safe to do so.

To escape the country for political reasons was a dangerous undertaking. Most comrades crossed the borders by foot into countries such as Namibia and Zimbabwe, and some traveled beyond the border states into countries such as Tanzania and Zambia. The journeys were fraught with natural hazards, and threat and fear of capture by police and informers. For my family, we were extremely lucky that our departure happened differently.

Death of My Father

To further compound all the strains on my family came the tragic loss of my father. On July 21, 1967, my father was killed mysteriously by a train in the Groutville area. Our family was devastated and has never been satisfied with the official explanation of the events of that day. The outpouring of grief spread throughout South Africa and was felt by us all. My father was memorialized at his place of worship, the small church close to our home, on July 29th. The government waived the apartheid laws so some 5,000 people, including diplomats and representatives of the Norwegian Nobel Committee, could attend the funeral.

Nomathuli and Nokukhanya Luthuli at Albert Luthuli's Funeral

Permission of Gcabashe Family

Thandi (second from left) with members of Luthuli family

Permission of Gcabashe Family

Planning the Departure—First Trip to the United States

One of the dignitaries at my father's service was William Redman Duggan, the American Consul General in Durban, who knew my father. Thulani and I became close friends with him and referred to him as "Red Duggan." He learned of our need to leave South Africa and offered to assist.

First, however, we needed passports, which were rarely issued to black Africans, as withholding travel rights from blacks was a means of control. The apartheid regime apparently thought that preventing us from having exposure to the outside world would prevent us from getting spoiled and making unnecessary demands.

To overcome the difficulty, Consul Duggan devised a plan to make use of the United States–South Africa Leader Exchange Program (USSALEP), which previously had been offered mostly to white South Africans, although some blacks had participated. As it required our having a passport, this was a means to obtain the necessary documents for our eventual immigration to America. Otherwise, we would probably never have left South Africa with our four children without encountering serious risks to our lives.

In 1969, Duggan extended the invitation to us to participate in the exchange program involving mostly speaking engagements. When the South African government rejected our candidacy, he threatened withdrawal of the entire program from South Africa. Duggan's threat was successful. Shortly thereafter, we were granted passports without a fuss, and in October 1969 we departed for the United States on a three-month program.

During our brief, three-month stay in the US, we scouted around for a city of our choice in which to raise our children. We considered three locations. We loved the vibrancy of Washington D.C., its politics and historical sites expertly described to us "VIPs." San Francisco was beautiful and picturesque and had a special appeal for its hilly topography not unlike Durban. It actually made me homesick and would have been a perfect choice were it not the experience of an earthquake while we were there. Atlanta won our hearts for a variety of reasons. It was comfortably small to raise our children without encountering problems of big city life. It had civil rights organizations and institutions such as the Southern Christian Leadership Conference (SCLC), the Martin Luther King Center for Nonviolent Social Change, the National Association for the Advancement of Colored People (NAACP), the Urban League, and many more. Other major draws to Atlanta were the strong religious culture of black churches and, in all honesty, the sizable black population. These brought us comfort.

We thought we would be able to leave for the visit much earlier and the delays resulted in challenges with the arrival of my fourth child, whom I wanted born in South Africa. Thankfully, however, my son Phakamele was born in South Africa, on December 26, 1969, shortly after we returned home.

Finalizing the Departure

We had planned to go into exile in the United States in June of 1970. That left us with six months to prepare to leave our beloved extended family and our country, not knowing if or when we could return home. This short preparation time was extremely busy and at the same time nerve-racking. We had to deny our reality. We had to maintain a veneer of normalcy and go about our lives as though nothing seismic was imminent. What we intended had to be kept as secret as possible.

A priority for me was to be a good mom to my newborn baby as well as my other three children, all still under six years of age. Our daily routine had to remain as normal as possible. Firstly, at their preschool, we could not have the children behave in a way that would make their teachers suspect something was amiss. Secondly, as children tend to boast to their play friends and by nature do not keep secrets, we had to talk and act discreetly around our kids. They could not know anything about our plans. Even with our extended family members, we were selective and cautious about whom to inform and when to do so, because—and this is a sad commentary on living under apartheid—we could not necessarily trust even our next of kin. Regarding my job with St. Aidan's, I was already on maternity leave, so nothing could raise suspicion there. Thulani kept his work schedule until the last moment.

During this time, the Special Branch kept hounding us. They wanted to confiscate our passports, so we played a triangulation game amongst Thulani, Consul Duggan, and me. When the Special Branch visited, they were referred to the other who was not home at the time. In the meantime, the documents were under lock and key at the American Consulate, which could not be raided due to diplomatic privilege.

We secretly sold our house in Clermont Township, or so we thought. Once in the United States we discovered, through sources, that our house had been sold to a government informant, so we realized the government probably knew of our plans. Why they let us leave South Africa is a mystery.

Our possessions could not be sold openly in a yard sale, so they were given away to family and friends or donated to welfare and charity organizations. Some things that I was sentimental about were entrusted to my sister, S'mangele Ndungan.

My husband quietly sold his legal practice to a trusted ANC lawyer.

The Departure

On the top-secret day of our departure in June of 1970, my mother came by herself to kiss the kids "bye-bye" and to bid us all farewell. She was clearly depleted emotionally, but stoically controlled herself and stood strong on our lawn singing, in solo, "God be with you till we meet again." She cut a lone but brave figure and I carried that solitary picture of her throughout exile. Even today I have tears as I recall that moment.

The only other presence that day was that of Consul Duggan and his wife, Bunny, who had been part of our exit plan for more than a year as it was hatched, processed, and refined. They provided us transportation to the Durban Airport.

In accordance with our agreement, if we were stopped on the way to the airport, the story line being this: the Consul and his wife were going on vacation and were accompanied by their domestic workers and family. In those days this was a common practice in South Africa. Luckily, and to our great relief, no stops occurred and we breathed easily on arrival at the airport. But this was only the first hurdle. Not until the immigration clearance was completed could the grip of panic and uncertainty let go of us.

My husband never stopped telling a joke about that critical juncture in the immigration departure process. The officials were Afrikaner and communicated with us only in Afrikaans, of which I was clueless. Fortunately, Thulani spoke fluently in their language. It was an emollient that flattered them and, on seeing their smiles, I knew things were going well. Most likely, without Thulani's mastery of Afrikaans, we might have been probed more intensively and in a roughshod style. The Afrikaner officials' interest in us was our reason for going to America. When we told them "to teach," they responded saying, "Tell those Americans good things about us." Of course, my husband gave a broad smile acknowledging their statement and we were done, having passed the test.

If I could, I might have sung, "Free at Last." But that was but one portion of our journey. We did not know what was ahead of us in exile.

Paris and London

Our itinerary took us to London via Paris. And what an onerous trip it was. The Orly Airport was extremely busy and crowded. I recall the haunting fear of losing one of the kids. Travel with four young children required some ingenuity so, in addition to both of us carrying hand luggage, my husband was responsible for the two older girls and I strapped the baby on my back and connected the two-year-old to my wrist. Hello! Africa had arrived in Paris. Keep in mind that strapping children on any part of the body had not yet become trendy in western culture, so I looked odd and different. But that was the least of my concerns.

London was a one-month stay with my sister, Albertina, who was already in exile there with her husband, Pascal Ngakane, and family.

Arrival in the US

We still did not have immigration papers to enter the United States. Consul Duggan had tried to speed up the process for our arrival, as he wanted it to occur in advance of the November 1970 USA national elections. There was a concern that the current Republican president, namely Richard Nixon, and a strengthened Republican Congress, would make it harder for us with an ANC background to pass through the USA immigration screening. As it turned out, in the elections the Democrats held on to the Senate majority and increased their majority representation in the House of Representatives.

Nevertheless, the Republican threat was not a myth. The ANC was classified as a terrorist, communist organization and the immigration questionnaires probed deeply and in a threatening manner in an attempt to weed out the "undesirable" visitors to the USA. If we were thought to be a threat to American security, permission to enter would be refused.

We were apprehensive but hopeful and relieved about starting our new life in Atlanta.

4
Atlanta, The Early Years:
Family, Work, and Activism, 1970-1981

Sponsorship, Welcome, and Support

In keeping with our plans, we flew from London via New York, our port of entry in the United States, and then to Atlanta's International Airport. United States law required that immigrants have sponsors and we were fortunate that Mrs. Coretta Scott King and Vincent Harding had agreed to serve in this role thanks in great part to our relationship with Consul Duggan.

With open arms and caring hearts, the Harding family—Vincent, his wife, Rose, and their children Rachel and Jonathan—welcomed my husband, our four children, and me at the airport. As Mrs. King was unable to be at the airport, the Hardings first took us to greet her at the Martin Luther King, Jr. Center, founded by Mrs. King in 1968 and for which she was the CEO and Vincent Harding was its director. During our earlier visit to the States in 1969, we had held discussions with the King Center about adding my father's papers, those that had survived the apartheid raids, to the King Archives. The MLK Center welcomed and consented to our request without hesitation, though the final result was their safekeeping at The Schomburg Center for Research in Black Culture in New York City.

The Hardings then drove us to their home where we remained for one year before we settled into our own place. The experience of having one of America's most prominent intellectuals, educators, and civil rights spokesmen to nurture, guide, and help us acclimate to our new life was a remarkable foundation upon which to start. The Hardings remained the guardians of our family for the duration of our time in Atlanta. They became, by proxy, the extended family we had left behind.

Another foundation that served to soften the disruption to our family life was the church. It was not just any church we joined, but the historic Central United Methodist Church with its Pastor, the Reverend Doctor Joseph L. Lowery, the iconic civil rights leader. His sermons, engrained with civil rights narratives, heightened our awareness of the links between the struggle in South Africa and that in the United States. I began to teach the Zulu culture and language to the congregation. In fact, Reverend Lowery asked me to introduce the Zulu greeting and this became a standard practice at the church. Our membership was perfect for us. My family, especially my children, found solace and refuge among the members of the congregation and gained friends for life as they grew into adulthood.

> **No.** 10244637
> **Name** GCABASHE, Tandi Hilda
> **residing at** Atlanta, Georgia
> **Date of birth** 8/13/34   **Date of order of admission** 6/29/70
> **Date certificate issued** June 14, 1977   by the
> U.S. District   **Court at** Atlanta, Georgia
> **Petition No.** 12536   **Alien Registration No.** A31 107 211
>
> T. Gcabashe
> (COMPLETE AND TRUE SIGNATURE OF HOLDER)

Thandi's USA Naturalization Document

Work, Home, and Raising My Children

When I married, I fully expected my life to be what every girl, even a South African girl, dreamed. It did not exactly happen that way. While I had hoped for an ordinary life, a good husband who would provide for and love me, children who were lovely, obedient, and smart, and a supportive extended family, that is not exactly what I got. Having children who are lovely, healthy, and smart is, of all the dreams, most important. My four children, without question, are my greatest accomplishments. They and my grandchildren are my life.

I do not question our decision to leave South Africa with our children and to make a life in America. It was the right thing to do. When I contemplate the alternative, I am frightened even from the safe distance of time. We were not alone in that thinking, especially after the Sharpeville Massacre of 1960, when so many young people and families were forced to flee for their lives. I was not alone in the belief that Atlanta would offer a desirable and reasonable alternative to the threat that South Africa represented to the wellbeing of one's family. The ranks of exiled

South Africans in Atlanta, which numbered less than 20 when I arrived in 1970, rose to more than 200 by 1990.

Thulani found work with an Atlanta bank as a corporate lawyer. He was there for many years and was the sole breadwinner for the family for the first several years. After my children had adapted well enough and I felt it was safe to leave them home alone, I sought and found work as a nurse at a neighborhood hospital in Atlanta in a position at a lower rank than my South African qualifications commanded. In order to gain full recognition, I needed to qualify in an American university, but the distance to classes and the cost proved too great. The same regulation applied to Thulani, who had to study for admission to the Georgia Bar, which he succeeded in doing.

Working on night duty in a community hospital close to my home, I found myself delivering a lot of babies. As they had in South Africa, I think the doctors made themselves unavailable at night knowing that I could "catch" the babies for them. Nurse midwives were a scarce commodity at that time. It was a time of not much sleep.

Thandi with Phakamele, Nokukhanya, Nomhle, Sibongile, and Friends

Permission of Gcabashe Family

The realities of life for an immigrant or a newcomer to a country not of one's birth quickly became apparent to me. Small things, yet exceptionally important ones, such as no credit history, became a hurdle. They prevented us from buying a house, a car, and furniture unless we could pay up front.

But eventually we were able to stand on our own, to purchase what was required to establish and run a full-fledged family home. The children enrolled in school, we were members of the Central United Methodist Church, and our family life assumed some semblance of normality. This, I thought, would be the course of our lives in America: normal, ordinary.

Beginning Activism

Part of assuming a normal life in Atlanta did involve creating a political life for Thulani and me. While it took us a while to decide our exact direction, a political life was normal for us, given our liberation work in South Africa. We were determined to have a visible South African presence in the city and were motivated to create the first ANC chapter in Atlanta.

At the time, in the 1970s, we were the only black South African family in Atlanta—that we were aware of, at least—yet there were a few South African students whom we rounded up for membership. All of them were attending Atlanta University and included Sehlare Makgetlaneng, Sifiso Makhathini, and Duma Gcabashe, our nephew, who had also chosen to live and study in Atlanta. All had a South African liberation, activist background and were unable to return to South Africa under the apartheid government. Ultimately, Makhathini, who was studying political science, became the chair of our local chapter, which was maintained until 1994, when the first democratic elections took place in South Africa.

In the 1980s, David Ndaba, Thabi, and their son Suku came to Atlanta from his ANC position with the Observer Mission to the UN in New York City. David had played a leading role in the Soweto Student Uprising in 1976 and, as a result, had to escape. He joined the local ANC chapter while studying at the Morehouse School of Medicine. Ultimately, David Ndaba (actual name was Dr. Sam Gulube) became the personal physician of former South African President, Thabo Mbeki, and later Secretary of Defense.

Another feature that launched us into our activist "normality" was the speaking engagements at the Atlanta University Center. Soon after we arrived, our presence and backgrounds became known. The opportunity to align with professors and students was significant then and in our later outreach. Anti-apartheid concerns and advocacy were already on their minds and in their actions. Thulani and I added but another component to what already existed, with the difference that we had had the direct experience of South African oppression under apartheid.

From this vantage point in the world of academia, our work extended to wider constituencies of support for South Africa's liberation. Our lives expanded down many and converging avenues as we began to associate ourselves with the church and with activist communities in Atlanta.

Through my church affiliation, thankfully, I was introduced to the larger Atlanta ecumenical community, and we gradually learned which of these religious institutions would willingly address and work against apartheid. They included black churches, and eventually the white churches of Methodists, Baptists, Quakers, and Catholics as well as Jewish synagogues, which were concerned about social and civil justice issues. Many welcomed dialogues about local and international justice. Atlanta also was home to conservative and fundamentalist churches, not all of which were interested.

Among both blacks and whites, we discovered little awareness about South African history, yet an eagerness to understand South Africa's apartheid system, and strategies to end it. Serious educational outreach was necessary. We were asked to speak to many groups in our first decade in Atlanta.

Nomhle (top), (right to left) Sibongile, Phakamele, and Nokukhanya

Permission of Gcabashe Family

Despite the demands of my job and occasional speaking engagements, I still maintained a firm grip on my children's development—prepared their meals, watched over their safety, and pushed them to keep their focus on their education. They were, in my eyes, doing well from all perspectives.

The family dynamics began to change by the late 1970s and early 1980s. My husband was never the nurturing type nor the disciplinarian. Eventually, Thulani ended his work with the bank and started an international import and export business that required his absence a large part of the time. I left the nursing profession and accepted a position in 1981 with the American Friends Services Committee as the Southern Africa Peace Education Director.

My eldest daughter, Sibongile, became quite the second mom to the remaining three and, in my absence, maintained order in the household. As a teen, she showed maturity and capability to manage household chores. I don't know how I managed the full-time job as a nurse except to say that Sibongile had to grow up very fast and bore the brunt.

These changes ultimately meant that both my husband and I were away often. My husband returned to South Africa permanently in 1983 and by that time we were living apart and never returned to the marriage. Sibongile was off to West Georgia College and our second daughter, Nomhle—responsible, academically inclined, and driven—was by 1984 enrolled at Emory University in Atlanta where she successfully matriculated. Our third daughter, Nokukhanya, was finishing high school and preparing to study at Howard University in Washington, DC. Also, by this time, Phakama (as he was called), the youngest was entering young manhood without the presence of his father, and without a male influence to usher him into that stage of life. This created a major crack in his future wellbeing. To grow up in America without his father, with a mother who was frequently absent because of work, and in an environment that was increasingly unforgiving of black males proved to be difficult for Phakama to navigate. He finished high school and was off to the Coast Guard for a few years. I felt better.

Part III

Liberation Struggle in Exile: My Anti-Apartheid Work

5

Partnerships:

My Father and Dr. Martin Luther King, Jr., US Civil Rights Leaders, US Anti-Apartheid Organizations, the United Nations

My Father and Dr. Martin Luther King, Jr.

Although my father and the Reverend Dr. Martin Luther King, Jr., never met in person, they corresponded with one another in the 1950s and 1960s. In 1957, Dr. King sent a letter to my father along with a copy of his book, *Stride Toward Freedom.* Together, on December 10, 1962, Human Rights Day, they issued their joint statement, *Appeal for Action against Apartheid*.

Appeal for Action Against Apartheid
Dr. Martin Luther King, Jr.
and Albert Luthuli

December 10, 1962

We, therefore, ask all men of goodwill to take action against apartheid in the following matter:

- Hold meetings and demonstrations on December 10, Human Rights Day;
- Urge your church, union, lodge, or club to observe this day as one of protest;
- Urge your government to support economic sanctions;
- Write to your mission to the United Nations urging adoption of a resolution calling for international isolation of South Africa;
- Don't buy South Africa's products;
- Don't trade or invest in South Africa;
- Translate public opinion into public action by explaining facts to all peoples, to groups to which you belong, and to countries of which you are citizens until an effective international quarantine of apartheid is established.

The statement called for adherence to the *UN Declaration of Human Rights* and asked that specific actions be taken to put pressure on the apartheid system. Together, they essentially demanded an isolation of the apartheid regime through broad economic sanctions. In issuing this call, both my father and Dr. King recognized that excessive violence of one group against another could lead to a racial war that "will destroy the potential for interracial unity in South Africa and elsewhere." It was a remarkable proclamation, which linked the civil rights movement in the United States and the anti-apartheid movement in South Africa.

The link they created demonstrated the widespread impact of European colonial oppression in Africa, its legacy in the United States, and how those persons most affected could join their efforts to end ongoing brutality. I learned from their example the significance of international solidarity on matters of justice and freedom. This was important to me and a lesson I attempted to implement in my own anti-apartheid work.

US Jim Crow and Apartheid Laws

There are powerful comparisons and striking parallels between the practices of legal racial segregation and economic discrimination in the US under Jim Crow laws and those of South Africa under the laws of apartheid. In both countries, the laws were accompanied by horrific intimidation, violence, and terrorist tactics. Jim Crow disenfranchised the black community through property, literacy, and tax requirements. Apartheid went further—no black South African was able to vote except under circumstances that had little impact on their lives. I inevitably brought these facts into my public talks, yet found for many Americans it was not easy to correlate the South African struggle for social, political, and economic justice with the struggle in the US.

Through descriptions by my father, I developed a familiarity with the southern part of the United States and with the US civil rights struggles. Upon arrival in the US, with Coretta Scott King and Vincent Harding serving as our sponsors, both my husband and I grew to understand at a deeper level the past and contemporary struggles for justice in the United States, in the South generally, and in Atlanta. We became familiar with many organizations and individual activists who had been involved in the United States, and in the South in particular, where the discriminatory laws prevailed more than any other part of the country. We were immersed in the knowledge and energy and history of the civil rights movement and by the activism of individuals and institutions. Having helped to ensure that the major accomplishments of the passage of the landmark legislation of the 1950s and 1960s—Brown vs. Board of Education (1954), the Civil Rights Act (1964), and the Voting Rights Act (1965)—implementing the legislation was another thing altogether. Activists, individually and collectively, were engaged in ensuring the implementation occurred. At the same time they were intrinsically and instinctively attuned to the parallels between the civil rights and anti-apartheid struggles, were already involved in efforts to end apartheid, and wanted to lend additional help.

Civil Rights Organizations in Atlanta Fighting Apartheid

The Martin Luther King, Jr. Center for Nonviolent Social Change, located on Auburn Avenue in Atlanta, was an important resource in any number of ways. Coretta Scott King and the King Family, along with other supporters, had created and then built the Center, whose primary mission was to teach Dr. King's nonviolence philosophy and strategies and to honor Dr. King through education and on-going civil rights advocacy, both locally and nationally. We came to consult and work closely together.

Further down Auburn Avenue was the headquarters of the **Southern Christian Leadership Conference (SCLC)**, which Dr. King and others created in 1957 after the 1955 Montgomery Bus Boycott. SCLC was to serve as the activist arm of the King-influenced ongoing civil rights movement. When I began my anti-apartheid work in 1981, SCLC's director was the Reverend Joseph Lowery, and the Reverend Timothy McDonald was its Program Director. Our connection was hugely important. Reverend Lowery's wife, Mrs. Evelyn G. Lowery, became my good friend. She created in 1979 the **SCLC Women's Organization for Movement for Equality Now, Inc. (W.O.M.E.N)** and I became head of its international program work.

The **Student Nonviolent Coordinating Committee (SNCC)** was founded in the 1960s by black and white youth to challenge the oppressive segregation policies and white supremacy in the South. The Reverend James Orange was one of the members who, together with Julian Bond and John Lewis, were active in Atlanta locally, and nationally in the on-going civil rights movement, as well as supporting our anti-apartheid work.

Created by 100 members of the clergy in 1965 to oppose the war in Vietnam, **Clergy and Laity Concerned (CALC)** evolved to engage in other issues. Its Atlanta chapter and director, the Reverend Emory Searcy, supported anti-apartheid work. Dr. King was one of the few blacks and the only clergy member from the South to attend the founding of Clergy and Laity Concerned in 1965 in New York City.

There is a consortium of historical black colleges and universities (HBCU) at the **Atlanta University Center,** initially composed of **Morehouse College, Spelman College**, **Clark Atlanta University, Morris Brown College,** and **the Interdenominational Theological Center.** Apartheid concerns and advocacy were already on their minds and our alignment with Atlanta University was significant throughout.

The long list of impressive activist students and professors who attended the Atlanta University colleges in the 20th century is quite remarkable: W.E.B. DuBois, Martin Luther King, Jr., Marian Wright Edelman, Whitney Young, Jr., Howard Zinn, Vincent Harding, Johnnetta Cole, and Mack Jones. The Atlanta University Center offered an opportunity for countless Africans from numerous countries to obtain their college degrees. This was also true for South Africans, as we soon learned.

It is an understatement for me to note that in Atlanta and other parts of the South, the black churches and their leaders were in many cases closely linked with civil rights activism. Atlanta is the home of many such churches, and civil rights leaders were pastors of these churches: The Reverend Ralph Abernathy, who became SCLC president after Dr. King, was the pastor of **West Hunter Baptist Church**; The Reverend Joseph Lowery, who became SCLC president in 1977, was the pastor of **Central United Methodist Church** and subsequently **Cascade Methodist Church.** The Reverend Timothy McDonald held a key position with SCLC as well with the **Concerned Black Clergy of Metropolitan Atlanta**.

In Atlanta, several black-owned radio stations, and the newspaper *The Atlanta Voice*, helped promote our work. There were also black and/or progressive radio stations such as **WCLK** (at Clark Atlanta University), **WAOK**, and **WRFG** (Radio Free Georgia) that disseminated information about speaking events and demonstrations.

Finally, and importantly, Atlanta was the first major city in the South to elect a black mayor, Maynard Jackson, in 1973. The Atlanta City Council was increasingly composed of black council members in the 1970s. This demonstrated the powerful black middle class and voting empowerment initiated and maintained by the black community. Atlanta black leader, Carl Ware, was elected to the City Council in 1973 and became the president of the Council in 1976, serving until 1979. He was the first black to hold such a position. Ware was later employed by Coca-Cola and it was Carl Ware whom I interfaced with, and sometimes confronted, in our efforts to urge Coca-Cola's divestment in South Africa. We became friends in spite of the confrontation.

There were white-led institutions and progressive whites who aligned themselves with the civil rights movement with whom we became familiar, namely, the **American Friends Service Committee (AFSC)**, the **Southern Regional Council**, the **American Civil Liberties Union (ACLU)**, labor unions, **Amnesty International,** the **Socialist Workers Party**, and numerous white churches.

Thus, in summary, we were surrounded by the knowledge and energy of the civil rights history and by the activism of individuals and institutions. These were perfect movement and organizing conditions. Many individuals, now legendary, and others less known were advocating for the end of apartheid. They were intrinsically and instinctively attuned to the parallels in the struggles, were already involved in efforts to end apartheid, and wanted to extend additional help. The existence of these individuals and their organizations were a blessing for the local, national, and international anti-apartheid movement.

The United Nations

The United Nations posthumously awarded my father the "United Nations Prize in the Field of Human Rights." This was in 1968, the first year the awards were presented. Thulani and I accepted the prize when we were first in the United States in 1969.

Throughout the decades, the UN's anti-apartheid resolutions censuring South Africa, and recommending embargos and sanctions to isolate South Africa, were critically important and influential to worldwide anti-apartheid efforts, including our own in Atlanta. E.S. Reddy and the **United Nations Special Committee Against Apartheid**, were particularly helpful supporting divestment campaigns as I later describe. Originally from India, Reddy served from 1963 to 1984, first as Principal Secretary of the UN Special Committee and later as Director of the UN Centre Against Apartheid.

UN Considerations and Resolutions (Partial)

1946-1950s	UN considers India's complaints of discrimination against Indians in South Africa and resolutions to consider South African government's racial policies
1961	General Assembly Resolution 1598 condemns apartheid
1963	Security Council resolution 181 and 182 to urge nations implement arms embargo against South Africa
1963-64	Security Council resolutions that Rivonia Trials end and political prisoners be released
1968	General Assembly requests all states to suspend cultural, educational, sporting, and other exchanges
1971	General Assembly resolutions calling for boycott of sport teams and protesting establishment of Bantustans and forced removal
1974	UN withdraws South Africa's credentials to the UN and provides observer status to the African National Congress and the Pan-Africanist Congress (PAC) as representatives of the South African people
1970s-80s	Security Council issues sanctions against South Africa and gives financial support to national liberation movements

US National Anti-Apartheid Organizations

On a consistent basis I conferred and collaborated with directors of US national anti-apartheid organizations throughout the years. Importantly, many of their leaders were black Americans, which reflected well on the concerns of black Americans.

The **American Committee on Africa (ACOA)/Africa Fund** in New York was often the leader in developing national work plans in consultation with other groups. Jennifer Davis, its director, was a white South African exile with a long history of anti-apartheid work inside and outside of South Africa. The Project Director was Dumisani S. Kumalo, a black South African who ultimately became the South African Ambassador to the United Nations under the Mandela presidency. I worked closely with both Jennifer and Dumisani.

The **AFSC's** national office was in Philadelphia, where its Southern African Program was coordinated by Jerry Herman, also a black American activist of long standing in the fields of civil rights and justice issues.

Begun in 1971, the **Interfaith Center for Corporate Responsibility (ICCR)** under the leadership of Timothy Smith, supported religious institutions as faith-based investors to urge corporate responsibility through divestment from South Africa.

TransAfrica in Washington was founded in 1977 with Randall Robinson, a black American attorney, as its first director. It was the catalyst for the Free South Africa Movement which drew major media and public attention to the anti-apartheid work.

These organizations and their programs were impressive. Their individual work was instructive and crucial for ours. It was wise for the anti-apartheid groups to work collaboratively and strategically together, and we did, expanding the breadth of outreach throughout the country. Coordinated initiatives and messages advanced our voice and our pressures on the national and international scene. We were doing difficult work, but it was made easier the more we worked together. The spirit of camaraderie even brought some fun on occasion. Talking about home and sharing other matters made us laugh.

There were religious and labor unions as well as many other informal groups who weighed in on countless actions. They were constant in their pressure on persons and institutions with authority, influence, and power—whether within Congress, corporate America, or educational institutions—to challenge through multiple approaches in order to bring down the apartheid system.

The work of the anti-apartheid groups in the US was purposeful in its support of a liberation movement that represented the aspirations of the people of South Africa. Additionally, and importantly, the programs we implemented were outlined and requested by the South Africans themselves, and shared with us by South African leaders in the international liberation struggle—largely through the ANC, as well as other liberation movements, such as the PAC. Given my affiliation with the ANC, then, I was able to incorporate many of its policies and requests into my work.

6
Affiliation with the African National Congress, Principles of Kingian Nonviolence

The people of South Africa had a long history of nonviolent struggle. From the time of the founding of the ANC in 1912, the leadership's approach was to reform peacefully the system of colonialism. Over the decades, the ANC progressed to a point where its Youth League pressured the elders to adopt its "Program of Action," wherein peaceful methods of struggle would be injected with a measure of militancy in disregard of apartheid laws. This led to the "Defiance of Unjust Laws Campaign" in 1952. At the peril of imprisonment, people volunteered to occupy public parks, trains, and post offices that had "Europeans Only" signs. Many trained volunteers registered for the campaign. Some gain accrued: a demonstrable increase in the ANC's membership from 7,000 to 100,000 and, for ordinary people, removal of the fear of confronting apartheid. In my opinion, this newfound confidence and attitude in black people spelled the beginning of the end of apartheid.

The ANC's armed wing was created in 1961 after the March 21, 1960 Sharpeville Massacre, in which 69 unarmed protestors opposing the apartheid government's pass laws were shot and killed by the Sharpeville police. The numbers included 10 children and 8 women and those fleeing the scene who were shot in the back. It was after this incident that many in the ANC decided they could no longer limit themselves to nonviolent protest. Umkhonto we Sizwe (Spear of the Nation), the armed wing of the ANC, was then launched.

My affiliation with the African National Congress became a point of conflict on occasion in the US, as the South African regime had designated the ANC as a terrorist and communist organization and many Americans concurred with that accusation as well. As a founder with Thulani of the Atlanta ANC Chapter, this presented some problems for me. I had always maintained my affiliation with the ANC, yet sometimes I had to separate myself from what the ANC was doing. The ANC

> **AFSC PERSPECTIVES ON NONVIOLENCE**
>
> in relation to groups struggling for social justice
>
> • Approved by the Board of Directors of the American Friends Service Committee January 24, 1981
>
> Permission of AFSC Archives

local chapter was neither organizing the armed struggle from Atlanta nor was it collecting funds for the armed struggle. Rather, the local chapter served as an educational and activist group to give the ANC a visible presence in Atlanta and the South.

These were issues I needed to address when first employed by the American Friends Service Committee, which is a Quaker organization deeply rooted in pacifism and the practice and promotion of nonviolent action in the search for peace and justice. Predating my employment, there had been a long discussion within the AFSC about whether to have a Southern Africa Program with South Africa and its liberation movements featured so prominently. Precisely because it is a Quaker organization, with a religious belief in nonviolence, support of a struggle for justice in which the leading group had resorted to armed military warfare was a difficult and worrying decision for the AFSC. The deliberation, self-assessments, and the final decision to support the Southern Africa Program predated my employment.

It's worth mentioning that the AFSC was not the only organization confronted by the issue of liberation movements that had incorporated violent means of struggle. The South African Council of Churches, as well as the World Council of Churches, underwent similar debates and self-examination. This was also the case in Atlanta.

I had to present all of the facts about the nature of the struggle to the American public, and those facts included the fact of armed struggle. After convincing the AFSC of the nature of my relationship with the ANC, I proceeded to say that "this is what the ANC is doing," describing the full scope of its resolve and efforts.

My communication with the ANC at first was difficult. Unlike other countries, the US did not have an official office for the ANC, though the UN in 1974 granted observer status to the ANC and the PAC. Over time in the 1980s, thanks partly to pressure from the anti-apartheid movement in the

> As the worldwide anti-apartheid movement grew in the 1970s and 1980s, the American Friends Service Committee became one of the key organizations linking U.S. activists with liberation movements in the region. Despite the continued pacifist commitment of the AFSC and its leading activists, strong personal ties facilitated an understanding of why the African movements felt compelled to turn to armed struggle. The ties built by the Lofts, the Tatums, the Bristols, and Bill Sutherland were strengthened, and the AFSC's Peace Education Division made anti-apartheid action one of its central programs. In "Nonviolence Not First for Export," James Bristol argued that activists in Western countries should understand the options open to movements in Africa. They should focus their own work on changing the policies of Western countries that supported the colonial and apartheid systems. "I believe in nonviolent revolution," he concluded, "but I also believe that it is neither humane nor practical to urge nonviolent revolution upon others whose situation is so totally different from our own."
>
> William Minter, *American Friends Service Committee and Africa: Vision and Action Over Five Decades* (AFSC, 2021)

US, an ANC representative was appointed to establish an office in New York City. Prior to that, I had communicated with the ANC head office in Zambia.

I did remain careful about what I could and couldn't do or say, when using the AFSC platform. Fortunately, the AFSC's educational and organizing program dovetailed with my own convictions. I was not against armed struggle, but I was not actively involved in it. Elizabeth Enloe, the Regional Director of the AFSC in Atlanta, was helpful along with Gloria Gaines, in advocating on my behalf on some of these issues with the AFSC headquarters in Philadelphia.

Needless to say, I never lost sight of the sensitivities surrounding this issue, which included the various positions within the ANC itself. There were many in the ANC who philosophically were not advocates of the military phase of our struggle, yet who intellectually accepted that all other means of peaceful struggle within South Africa had been exhausted and, consequently, the resort to violence had become inevitable.

The connection between Atlanta and South Africa was strong in regards to the history of strategic planning and nonviolent social change. Mahatma Gandhi had begun his journey as a nonviolent activist when he was forcibly removed from a train designated for whites in South Africa. Gandhi's influence on Dr. King had also influenced many of us in South Africa.

Kingian Nonviolence Principles

1. Once the problem is identified, it is essential to research the issue (i.e., define the problem, who the key players are, and who or what is being affected). The research and analysis should be above reproach, as disputed or incorrect facts and figures can completely undermine the efforts for the evolving campaign.

2. Based on the research, state clearly what needs to change in order to solve the problem, then identify the strategy for solving the problem.

3. Recruit others to join the struggle, share your findings and strategies, get their input if necessary, but essentially seek a commitment from them (e.g.: This is the problem. This is what we intend to do. Are you with us?).

4. Teach them nonviolent tactics (e.g., being non-confrontational during direct action).

5. Attempt to resolve the problem through negotiations (i.e., negotiations with whoever controls the policies needing to be changed).

6. If that doesn't work, apply pressure through direct action techniques, which at times need to be sustained for a lengthy period (i.e., boycotts, mass demonstrations).

7. Negotiate again. If necessary, engage in direct action again. Often, more research is required or more clarity as to the solutions that need to be developed.

8. Finally, if the problem is solved, seek reconciliation.

Of lasting importance to me was the influence of my father's views, discussed around the dinner table in my youth and echoed in the discussion of "Kingian Nonviolence" while living with the Harding family. Over the years of friendship with Vincent, we had many discussions on nonviolent principles and social change strategies and the Kingian "steps." As they were foundational and heavily influenced my work, we applied almost all of Dr. King's nonviolent principles and steps to our anti-apartheid work.

7

Beginnings of Anti-Apartheid Work as a Full Time Endeavor, 1981-1983

AFSC Southern Africa Peace Education Program

In the late 1970s, the American Friends Service Committee had begun Atlanta-based work on Southern Africa and posted an advertisement for volunteers. Both Thulani and I decided to answer the ad and offer assistance. Little did I know then that I was beginning a long journey with the AFSC and the US anti-apartheid movement, a journey whose breadth and depth I could not have predicted.

Permission of AFSC Archives

AFSC, an international Quaker organization with a record of early opposition to apartheid, had published the highly regarded book entitled *South Africa: Challenge and Hope*, enjoyed a long association with peoples on the African continent, and maintained commitments to education, divestment, and sanctions. It supported humanitarian relief and community-based development efforts throughout the world, and in the southeastern United States was known for its work with migrant populations and its support of civil rights.

In the summer of 1981, AFSC asked me to temporarily fill the staff position left vacant when Herbert Katedza returned to Zimbabwe. I shortly thereafter applied for the permanent position and by August of 1981 the

AFSC completed its process and formalized my appointment as Program Director for its Southern Africa Peace Education Program in the Southeast.

Pressure was building throughout the world as international solidarity mounted to bring an end to apartheid. The United States was seeing a mushrooming of anti-apartheid initiatives by legislators in the US Congress, in state and city assemblies, by students, by national organizations, and by local activists. There had been success on college campuses and in corporate board rooms at convincing universities and corporations to sell off their investments in South Africa. The anti-apartheid movement was visibly active and escalating in strength in parts of the US, particularly in the Northeast and on the West Coast. The movement was less prominent in the southern states, which were still deeply embedded in the historical struggle of racial integration and in the prosecution of the recent major civil rights legislation.

The AFSC's emphasis was public education on Southern Africa, in order to elevate awareness of apartheid, build interest in sanctions and divestment, and focus attention on the conditions in countries neighboring South Africa. What needed to be done, in the demographics of the nine-state region, fell on my shoulders and I was ready.

The volunteer AFSC Program Committee, on which I had served earlier, eagerly gave serious shape and substance to the program. Members of the Political Science departments of the Atlanta University Center were instrumental in helping launch our educational emphasis. Mack Jones, Earl Picard, and Shelby Lewis joined Noel Erskine, Maria Ladd, Bettye Ligon, Carol Luther, Isaac Miller, and Elizabeth Siceloff on the Committee.

Permission of AFSC Archives

Within a short period of time, we had concretized the program's goal and objectives, as well as the strategies of massive public education, coalition building with like-minded organizations, creation of local anti-apartheid groups throughout the southeast, and community mobilization in an array of actions.

Simply stated, our goal was to end the system of apartheid and assist the people of South Africa to establish a truly democratic, multi-racial society and government. This required the termination of US support for apartheid and the establishment of a just US foreign policy toward all Southern Africa nations oppressed by apartheid.

Within the first two years of my work, by 1983, the Southern Africa Program had succeeded in developing its key program areas.

Invitations to speak on South Africa were on the increase from communities throughout the southeastern states and I had started my multiple speaking engagements while making arrangements in the nine states to supply speakers and workshop personnel.

Jerry Herman, AFSC national staff person for South Africa, and I enjoyed direct contact with the national anti-apartheid organizations—the American Committee on Africa, the Washington Office on Africa, and TransAfrica. We were included in on-going strategic discussions.

Thandi and Dumisani Kumalo with Many Key Anti-Apartheid Activists,
AFSC National Office

Permission of Jerry Herman Collection

At the local level, we had developed constructive working relationships with The Martin Luther King, Jr. Center for Nonviolent Social Change. We were guests of Mrs. King for meetings with US national black leaders and with US Congressional legislators attending conferences at the Center, and we were invited to co-host the visits of South African personages such as Albertina Sisulu and Bishop Desmond Tutu. The opportunity to engage with King Center summer interns studying nonviolence and the civil rights movement was particularly important to me.

We had partnered with the staff of the Southern Christian Leadership Conference, whose divestment and boycott work well were underway. So too were the missions of other partner organizations upon whose leadership we could rely on to engage their membership in anti-apartheid organizing and educational initiatives—the National Association for the Advancement of Colored People, PUSH, the Atlanta

Permission of AFSC Archives

Christian Council, Amnesty International, Clergy and Laity Concerned, and Concerned Black Clergy among others.

We were in close communication with the ANC, PAC, Black Consciousness Movement and other South African liberation groups to assure our contribution was relevant to their struggle and was responding to needs they identified.

Annual events were becoming major educational undertakings in commemoration of Black History Month, the Sharpeville Massacre, the Soweto Uprising, and Political Prisoners Day. The Sharpeville commemoration, for example, was marked by two weeks of public rallies, films, teach-ins at the Atlanta University Center along with a letter writing campaign in support of South African bills before the US Congress.

Bill Sutherland's visit in November 1982 followed two AFSC educational tours in the South. As a renowned African American pacifist who had forged links between Americans and the African liberation struggle for decades, Bill inspired program supporters, especially those who were unsure and not yet totally committed.

Georgia Coalition for Divestment in South Africa

Crucial and significant among the accomplishments in those first two years was the emergence of the Georgia Coalition for Divestment in South Africa as a major anti-apartheid player in Atlanta.

Two months after my start with the AFSC, I placed an advertisement in *The Atlanta Voice* announcing a public gathering on a Saturday morning in October 1981 to share information on Southern Africa. About twenty-five people convened at the First Congregational Church on Courtland Street and John Wesley Dobbs Avenue in downtown Atlanta. It was an excellent start to our community organizing efforts. I stressed the need for individuals who would be willing to share their time and talents in working with me. Participants immediately formed a committee, distinct from the AFSC's Program Committee, including the professors from Atlanta

Georgia Coalition for Divestment in South Africa

Vision - free South Africa from apartheid rule.

Goal - assist South Africans to eliminate the system of apartheid and replace it with a democratically elected government on the basis of an unqualified universal franchise.

Mission - raise the awareness of the American people about the plight of black South Africans and about apartheid, a unique brand of racism legalized by the national government.

University Center with whom I was already working, and Gloria Gaines, who had contacted me upon her seeing the ad and met me for lunch. Gloria had recently returned to Atlanta from Nigeria, where she had been introduced to the struggle in South Africa. She was committed and energetic and a perfect leader. She became my good friend.

Having initially organized as The Southern Africa Support Committee members ultimately adopted the name Georgia Coalition for Divestment in South Africa (GCDSA). They developed a structural framework well-designed for various activities and a business plan to guide the work. They got busy using the AFSC office as the center of gravity for coalition activities. Mack Jones and Gloria Gaines joined forces as the co-chairs.

Membership grew in leaps and bounds, with genuinely committed individuals from a wide range of backgrounds. We succeeded in gathering people who might not have collaborated otherwise—people of disparate political beliefs, race, ethnicity, economic class, faith, age, and profession, from university staff and students, churches, labor unions, the civil rights movement, as well as state and city government officials. People came forward to assist and we honored them for their interest. We offered opportunities to contribute in ways that matched their talents and expertise. Everyone was valued.

Coalition members investigated banks and corporations in Atlanta that were engaged in business in South Africa; assisted in the preparation of divestment legislation bills for submission to Atlanta City Council and the Georgia General Assembly; and disseminated information through teach-ins, lectures, and public rallies. The Coalition introduced the Cultural Boycott to Atlantans.

Program Resources, Colleagues, and Volunteers

I worked with twelve volunteer members of the AFSC Program Committee in addition to program staff when funds permitted, among whom were Kuhuzu Wanzu, Moriba Karimoko, Makini Coleman, Malkia M'Buzi Moore, and Soter Irusota. There were fifty to sixty volunteer members of the Georgia Coalition on Divestment in South Africa, and small groups of volunteers in the various cities.

The 1983 annual budget was $23,490. Funds to expand the Program's outreach were and would remain throughout the years the most critical organizational problem we faced. I was and remained the only staff person of any organization to address apartheid and Southern Africa issues on a full-time basis in the southern part of the United States.

On the question of leadership responsibilities, I simply add that whatever skills I employed were learned from my father. At home, I had not been reluctant to enter the thick of the struggle against apartheid, in a supportive role—not a leadership role as the work now demanded. It may come as a shock to some of my colleagues and friends that I had never addressed a public meeting or rally.

AFSC Southeast Regional Office Retreat, North Carolina
Front row: Thandi, Terry Sorelle, Elizabeth Enloe
Middle: Bob Brister, Jon Fried, unidentified staff
3rd row: unknown male, Kathy Hirsh, Peter Upon, unidentified staff
4th row: Zoharah Simmons, Debra Brooks, Marianela Jauregui
Top: Kuhusu Wanzu, Martha McDonald

Permission of AFSC Archives

Thandi with Event Participant at AFSC Offices

Community Activists, Gary Washington and Nomhle Gcabashe Standing at Right
Shafeah M'Balia Sitting at Right

Thandi with AFSC Atlanta Office Colleagues
Front row: Marina Riadi, unidentified person, Fulani Sunni Ali,
AFSC volunteer, Thandi
Back row: Almaz Tedla and Moriba Karamoko

Permission of Elizabeth Enloe

Coalition of Conscience Bracelet Project

Craig Shelton in Thandi's Office

8

Apartheid's Ongoing Atrocities

I had entered the decade of the 1980s, which evolved into probably the darkest days in South Africa, with the South African government engaged in atrocities more fully described below, and in attempts at sham reforms which sowed confusion at home and in the international community. It was helpful that we were clear—we were never about reforming apartheid, but dismantling it. Had we been unclear, we could have easily vacillated and digressed.

Over the years there arose occasions for critical thinking and critical decision making. At such times, in concert with my Program Committee and the Georgia Coalition, tough decisions were taken even when such decisions differed from the perspectives of influential persons. The decision to demonstrate at the Atlanta concert of Paul Simon with Ladysmith Black Mambazo was one example, and a second was the decision to declare and implement a boycott of Coca-Cola products.

Government Retaliation to Opposition

Intensification of events in South Africa gave shape to the program. Ongoing opposition to the apartheid laws within South Africa followed by government retaliation through renewed brutal attacks and harassment—physical assaults, killings, detentions, and imprisonment without trials, bannings, closing of clinics and schools—was gaining more visibility in the world press.

In 1985, the government of President Botha tried to counter the democratic movement in-country and respond to mounting international pressures by declaring a partial state of emergency. It was followed in 1986 by a full State of Emergency, ushering in a harsh crackdown.

At the same time, there were clandestine death squads operating in the South African security forces. The regime continued to resort to assassinating leaders such as had been done to Steve Biko in 1977. An often-overlooked case is that of my friend, Dulcie September, whose political commitment to the struggle and to the rights of women ended in Paris in March 1988 when she was shot five times by an unknown shooter. Later there was the assassination of Chris Hani, in April 1993, by a right-wing extremist. Hani was a staunch Umkhonto we Sizwe member and leader of the South African Communist Party who had great leadership potential.

External Raids on Frontline States

In the 1970s, opposed to the establishment of black rule in the white-dominated countries of Angola, Mozambique, and Rhodesia, South Africa had given military assistance to whites there which proved to be unsuccessful. The government's attempt at regional domination continued after these countries had achieved their independence. An example of the regime's offenses is a 1982 raid in Lesotho against the homes of alleged ANC members in the residential areas of Maseru, which resulted in the deaths of 42 people, of whom 30 were reported to be South African refugees while 12 were local civilians, including 7 women and children. Three of those killed had been prisoners on Robben Island. South Africa claimed that they attacked operatives who had been sent to assassinate two Bantustan leaders and 12 others who operated the command center to plan and execute guerrilla activities. The raid heightened tensions between Lesotho and South Africa while sharpening divisions within Lesotho.

In 1986, the South African Defense Force attacked Zambia, Botswana, and Zimbabwe simultaneously as the South Africans hosted an international peace delegation.

In 1987, South Africa launched an unsuccessful war in Angola, to topple a Marxist government, to gain strategic military advantage, and to install a more compliant government to control Angola's vast oil reserves. Cuba came to the defense of Angola and forced South Africa to retreat, not so much from its regional ambition, which was to still be the dominant force, but from the immediate goals of neutralizing a hostile regime that would give sanctuary to the South West Africa People's Organization and capturing a mineral-rich prize.

President Botha's Reforms

Before his downfall, P.W. Botha had made several attempts to reform apartheid so that it could survive. He proposed that blacks be allowed to buy their homes, that more freedoms be accorded to trade unions, and that more money be spent on black education. He also repealed the Prohibition of Mixed Marriages Act and relaxed some pass laws and employment restrictions. More controversially, Botha's government moved to operationalize the homelands policy, which proved his insincerity, since the purpose of that policy was to remove blacks from the citizenship rolls and secure white minority rule.

Botha's failure to tamp down the internal opposition to apartheid proved the failure of his approach. By 1989, many in the National Party had lost confidence that Botha could deliver, and Botha was replaced by F.W. de Klerk as State President.

All this activity and series of unfolding events throughout the years set the stage for and gave shape to our efforts to educate US constituents and further isolate the apartheid government. We in the southern part of the United States were poised to add pressure and influence.

Thandi (Second from Left) with Panelists

Permission of AFSC Archives

9
Education, Education, Education

Public Speaking Engagements

We were in the business of education. Our program's core purpose was the expansion of public awareness of apartheid on a massive scale. Action required knowledge; education was called for to mobilize US public support.

While the history and realties of South Africa were becoming increasingly known, there remained a dearth of awareness among many Americans, including social activists. So, too, the correlation between the long struggle to end apartheid and the struggle for racial equality in the United States, while clear to many, was not apparent or meaningfully obvious to most.

We answered as many speaking requests as possible. Our initial opportunities were in Georgia, Alabama, and Tennessee, but by 1983 we had begun solid work in Greensboro and Charlotte, North Carolina; in Jackson and Oxford, Mississippi; in New Orleans, Louisiana; and in Tallahassee, Florida. The program, designed to serve a nine-state region, eventually extended nationally as we received invitations from throughout the country.

The work necessitated extensive travel on my part to hundreds of engagements. Rarely did I decline an invitation. Sometimes I was accompanied, sometimes I traveled with a group, but most of the time I traveled alone. It was satisfying but also tough work, sometimes under undesirable conditions, and almost always with a tight expense budget. The map pinpoints the extent of my travel. Often my written reports suffered a low priority, but the record available to remind me, combined into an appendix, reflects that over the course of the years, invitations came for talks, speeches, keynote addresses, panel presentations, debates, and public rallies from audiences in more than a third of the fifty states. Many times there were multiple engagements in each site, and my report of the audience size I inevitably recorded as "small" or "large."

Thandi speaking in Seattle, Washington, 1985

Permission of Estate of Selma Waldman

Speaking Engagements Sites in US

Map by Laura McIntyre

I carefully and painstakingly explained the following basic and substantive issues to my audiences:

- **Apartheid laws and their consequences,** enacted by the all-white South African parliament to systematically discriminate, humiliate, impoverish, and imprison the non-white population for the perceived benefit of white South Africans
- **Biblical rationalization of the existence of apartheid laws** via interpretation of the story of Noah's son Ham—the so-called "curse of Ham"—used to explain black skin, substantiate slavery, and claim the God-given primacy and superiority of white people to rule over inferior blacks
- **Similarities between the racially discriminatory apartheid and the US Jim Crow laws,** including striking parallels of terrifying injustices and intentional cruelty
- **American business investments and profit-making in South Africa,** which supported the apartheid regime through payment of corporate taxes, which in turn were used to purchase strategic technology, assure essential oil production, and strengthen the auto industry, including military hardware and equipment designed to enforce conformity among—or kill—black people
- **International companies in South Africa playing the role of apartheid agents** when conducting passbook inspections of workers and reporting non-compliance to the South African authorities
- **The US foreign policy of "constructive engagement,"** biased towards the apartheid regime, favored by President Reagan and, by extension, by many

members of Congress, state legislatures, and local city councils
- The **Comprehensive Anti-Apartheid Act,** making its way through various committees and houses of the US Congress; and similar state and local sanction legislation
- **Turmoil and oppression by South Africa against African independence movements in Southern Africa—the "frontline states"**—through legislation and dehumanization (South Africa, Namibia) or destabilization by bombing and economic pressures (Angola, Mozambique, and Zimbabwe)

Slideshows, films, and documentaries accompanied these public talks, and question-and-answer periods inevitably followed, with animated discussion. In the early years, it was not uncommon for my children to set up and run the equipment for any number of films which awakened understanding of apartheid. Here is a small sampling:

- *The Long March* (trade union organizing, 1986)
- *Amandla: The Struggle for a Country* (1982)
- *You Have Struck a Rock* (women's contributions and campaigns, 1981)
- *Cry for Freedom* (Namibia, 1981)
- *A Luta Continua* (Mozambique, 1971)
- *Generations of Resistance* (1980)
- *Banking on South Africa* (1977)
- *South Africa and US Global Corporations* (1976)

Last Grave at Dimbaza

One documentary particularly shocked every audience. *Last Grave at Dimbaza* (1974) depicts the availability of cheap, exploitable black labor in support of the privileged and luxurious lifestyle of white South Africans. A white madam is able to hire three or four servants, often including a gardener, chauffeur, or butler. The servant responsible for a white baby is the child's sole caretaker, providing love, stimulating exercises, and nutritious meals. Yet, regardless of the close bond that inevitably develops between the child and the nanny, as the child grows so does their estrangement, and the cycle of racism perpetuates.

The film's most heartbreaking feature is the acute contrast between the white child and the nanny's own baby, being raised by the grandmother in a distant, deplorable, impoverished Bantustan. The liquid in this baby's bottle is a solution made from ground corn cooked in water with sugar added. Invariably, this baby develops kwashiorkor with the characteristic distended stomach and body edema. This child, and all other babies so affected, dies before five years of age. Because of the number of such children, the graves are dug in advance, row after row, in readiness for burial.

Although I had witnessed this reality many times back home, I too, at first viewing of the film, experienced the deep emotional reaction of all audiences—tears, shock, and difficulty participating in the question-and-answer period.

News Media—TV, Radio, and Print Media

I recruited support to the anti-apartheid movement, the issues, and the program through numerous opportunities for TV and radio appearances and talks with journalists eager for perspectives and quotes to enhance their stories. The print media covered our work occasionally and were interested in my views, which I was pleased to offer. Print news, and TV and radio appearances extended our reach.

"Jumping from the Frying Pan into the Fire"

Individuals were incredulous that apartheid was possible. It was not uncommon for people to react with disbelief. In most instances, the audience's engagement was rewarding. Most Americans responded as though the issues were their own problem. Most immediately wanted to become involved and we suggested organized ways to do so.

Then, too, on occasion we were met with hostility. Serious insults, derogatory epithets, and threats were hurled at me—and others in our program in separate instances—by a few unruly groups during question-and-answer time. Individuals would call Africans barbaric and ignorant and invoke Tarzan images and caricatures. The insults and insinuations would suggest that had white Europeans not come to Africa we still would be living in caves, and that the vast wealth of our continent would not have been explored and exploited. At times we were even labeled as being communists.

My first such encounter was in Florida when I was on tour alone. After experiencing grueling insults at the conclusion of my presentation, the most intimidating aspect of the whole experience was the drive to the home of the woman who had invited me and was to host me overnight. We traveled in the dark through vast, open, uninhabited tracts of land, late at night, not knowing if we were being followed.

Another occasion stands out. I was invited by concerned parents of a racially mixed high school in Oxford, Mississippi, in 1983, to refute an earlier talk given by a white South African student during Black History Month. In her presentation, sponsored by the South African Rotary Club, the student showed a video of black South African women with exposed breasts and faces smeared with a red make-up. She had apparently commented saying, "You see how barbaric they are? We can't be expected to associate with them."

I felt uneasy when the vice-principal drove me to the school from the airport. We passed Mississippi University where I observed a football game in progress not far from the high school. It was this same university that an African American, James

Meredith, in 1962, initially blocked from entering, was escorted onto the campus by federal marshals in order to enroll. Such games at the University had a reputation of becoming racially charged and this game was no different. Apparently, in lieu of the customary singing of the national anthem at the game, the "Ole Miss" audience instead sang "Dixie"—and the Confederate flag was flown. The black football players had refused to play that day. The dispute escalated and white students hung the offensive flags from their dormitory and car windows and made loud, incessant hooting of car horns everywhere in the campus vicinity.

I was cordially received and welcomed by the principal and the mostly black parents who had invited me. The students were instructed to thread the film I had brought with me. They returned in a panic from the auditorium, running into the office, screaming that angry, white parents had ripped the film apart and were threatening to deal with anyone coming to the presentation. In a short while, there was a confrontation between the black and white parents.

The principal whisked me out of the school, back to the airport. That was my ugly, scary, and rude awakening to racism in the southern United States.

The irony in this incident was that back home some of the few close family members who knew about our exile plan had said that we were "jumping from the frying pan into the fire'" in choosing Atlanta as our home.

The incidents were rare but memorable. The fact was that in Atlanta and in other metropolitan cities in the South it was surprisingly uncommon for me to encounter race-related problems. Rural areas were different.

I experienced up close and personally the history of black struggles in the United States while I organized against South African apartheid. Always I found it staggering how many in the US once characterized American blacks as uneducated and unable to govern and denied them the right to vote in their own country.

Even though I had known about these parallels in attitudes and policies, the details repeatedly appeared before me.

Proponents of South Africa's Apartheid

We forged ahead against seemingly unremitting, intransigent proponents of the apartheid regime who defended South African policies. The South African government was sending representatives to the United States to counter anti-apartheid work, adding credence to some Americans' preconceived, negative perceptions of black South Africans. Propaganda in public schools, such as that in Oxford, was a major concern of our program. The representatives were often effective. They were able to imbue some people's minds with the apartheid ideology of the primitive, inferior, and violent African.

There were even some South African liberals speaking in the international arena who articulated the unreadiness of black South Africans for a full and total franchise. They described blacks as uneducated, illiterate, and without property ownership. It was a no-win situation. The Bantu education laws undermined any semblance of equality and doomed blacks in South Africa to never qualify for full franchise.

We certainly had our educational work cut out for us.

US Regional Speaking Tours

The AFSC organized regional educational tours throughout the US, promoting person-to-person dialogue with high-level experts on Southern Africa. They addressed a wide array of audiences in multiple states during a single tour with the assistance of local organizers.

One of these tours—my first—was in the planning stages of activities by the AFSC's national office for the Fall of 1981 when I accepted the position in Atlanta. The tour successfully brought together representatives of SWAPO, ANC, Defense and Aid Fund, Campaign to Oppose Bank Loans to South Africa, and Washington Office on Africa to speak in the southeast US—in Virginia, North Carolina, Alabama, Mississippi, Louisiana, Florida, and Georgia. A second AFSC-sponsored tour in 1984 sent teams of four to twenty cities in the southeast.

In 1986, the Africa Peace Tour, a multi-organizational endeavor of twelve organizations including the AFSC, ended its twenty-eight-day national tour in Atlanta with several engagements. I participated in the southern wing of the tour, speaking in Miami and Gainesville, Florida as well as in the Atlanta events.

Heather Gray was instrumental in organizing the 1987 Africa Peace Tour which enabled African and American activists to speak in seven southeastern states. The tour's emphasis included South Africa's assault and wars on neighboring countries, a reality we never failed to address. I was one of thirty participants, along with Josh White Jr. (singer in the Sun City video), Jean Sindab (Director of the Washington Office on Africa), James Oporia-Ekwaro (past Executive Secretary of the All-Africa Council of Churches), Ezekiel Pajibo (student leader from Liberia), and George Shepherd (professor of International Relations, University of Denver).

Another tour launched in Atlanta in 1993 with a three-day orientation. Twenty delegates from Angola, Zaire, Tanzania, Mozambique, Somalia, and South Africa offered insight and analysis of events in their respective countries. The tour covered twenty-two cities in the southeast region. Atlanta activities included presentations at churches and schools, on television and radio programs, at an editorial board meeting, and a round table discussion at The Carter Center. Each delegate gave an insightful analysis of events in their respective countries.

When Atlanta was a destination, we in the AFSC office undertook the local planning and arrangements for all the speaking engagements. Such tours consumed mountainous amounts of staff time to organize, and we reaped much good for our program's education and community engagement objectives.

Travel Conditions

Being on tour was often not easy for me. In our travels we frequently stayed in the homes of those who supported our work. Given our non-profit organization budgets, the hotels were invariably too expensive and home accommodations were accepted.

Not all homes could accommodate us reasonably or comfortably. Often, we slept on a sofa or on the floor in the living room in spaces occupied by a dog or cat. I am asthmatic and animal hair usually precipitates an asthmatic attack. Pro-steroid pills helped to prevent impending attacks, for otherwise I would be incapacitated and unable to participate. I came to realize that ultimately being uncomfortable on occasion was all a part of organizing. There was virtually nothing that was going to stop me from doing the work.

US Elections—Primaries and Caucuses: 1984

I had the opportunity to participate in the Iowa state caucuses in January of 1984, which would later help select a party's presidential nominee. This was the year the incumbent, President Ronald Reagan (Republican), ran and won in November against his Democratic opponent, former Senator Walter Mondale. The long, drawn-

1984 Iowa Caucus Tour. Thandi with Matthew Walker and Brooke Baldwin of Coalition Against Apartheid, Yale University

Permission of Jerry Herman Collection

out election process was unlike that of any other country I knew.

The AFSC staff tracked aspiring political candidates' views on apartheid and, with representatives of other anti-apartheid groups, traveled to various states during election primaries or caucuses to pose questions publicly to candidates, mostly to men, regarding their understanding and positions. Direct access was usually difficult for security reasons, so our questions were most frequently relayed through reporters who were well versed and interested.

Iowa is an agricultural state and it snowed heavily when we were there. Our male host lived alone, welcomed us warmly, and had prepared and served us a sumptuous dinner of roast lamb. While praising the succulent meal, I asked for "seconds." Our host responded by saying that the young lamb we were eating had been sick with a fever and he decided to finish it off before it died on its own. Wow! What a bombshell for the two students from Yale University who had asked for seconds as well. They hastily cancelled their order, but I went ahead to eat my serving. I had been served already and I had heard my Mom say exactly the same thing before slaughtering a chicken or turkey.

Commemorative Events

The Georgia Coalition selected historical dates to commemorate which were largely those days observed by the United Nations and the Organization of African Unity. Each of these commemorations grew naturally into major, annual education opportunities held in Atlanta into the 1990s and requiring a lot of careful planning.

South Africa Awareness Week (February)

By the 1970s, US Black History Month was well established in the United States. Our contribution developed and over the years would become "Southern Africa Awareness Week" extending its scope beyond South Africa to neighboring nations. This annual event grew in scope so that by the second year, in 1988, we were scheduled for over twenty events in Atlanta.

Sharpeville Massacre (March); Soweto Uprising (June)

South Africa's regime of brutality and violence against unarmed citizens unleashed extensive international responses. We organized annual commemorations of the Sharpeville Massacre of March 21, 1960, and the Soweto Student Uprising of June 16, 1976, to honor the memory of the victims, their convictions, and their stance against the oppressive apartheid system.

These commemorations extended into two weeks of public rallies, teach-ins at Atlanta University Center, displays and distribution of literature, and letter writing and telegram campaigns in support of the South Africa bills before the US Congress and the Georgia Assembly.

During our 1986 Soweto 10-Year Commemoration, I was participating in a conference in Toronto and flew home to take part in the Solemn Meeting for Freedom in South Africa at the Atlanta University Center. Fred Dube of the ANC was in Atlanta attending the Human Dignity Forum and agreed to speak, along with representatives of our partner organizations—Concerned Black Clergy, Atlanta Christian Council, Clergy and Laity Concern, American Federation of Teachers, Amalgamated Transit Union, and others.

Distinguished Visitors
Leah Tutu–November 1985

Leah Tutu accepted the invitation of our AFSC national office, and I accompanied her during her November 1985 three-week speaking tour in the US. She addressed audiences in New York City, Philadelphia, Washington, DC, Atlanta, and Jackson, Mississippi.

Leah's presence in both Atlanta and Jackson excited the interest of the press, young people, and notable friends and partners of the civil rights movement. A gracious woman, she spoke her beliefs eloquently during press conferences, meetings with editorial staff, a gathering of youth representatives of organizations opposing apartheid, university students, and at large public events, the largest drawing over 2,000 people at the King International Chapel at Morehouse College. She called for economic sanctions and divestment, described the oppression of South Africa's domestic workers, explained growing frustration and violence, refuted the assertion of the automatic choice of communism by the liberation movement, and urged the US and other western nations to pressure the South African apartheid regime to abandon an "evil policy."

Overall, the press was accurate in reporting her comments, though some were mired in the concern of a communist threat. The *Atlanta Journal*'s headline was: "Mrs. Tutu: Soviet help is acceptable." The Georgia Coalition challenged the *Atlanta Daily World's* editorial in a five-page rebuttal.

Managing Leah's schedule and the desires of those wishing a private audience required our best diplomatic skills. We kept her needs foremost and wished to protect her time, yet found her graciously acceding to schedule additions. In her own right, Leah was a powerful spokesperson for a country free of racial conflict. Mayor Andrew Young proclaimed November 7th, 1985 Leah Tutu Day in Atlanta.

"I can't understand why it's so difficult for people, who have fought for freedom and got it, to understand that South African blacks want it."

"We are grateful for the support we are receiving from the American public, but we need great pressure from your government on the government of South Africa."

Leah Tutu, November 1985

86   Thandi: Liberation

Leah Tutu and Coretta Scott King

Standing: Coretta Scott King and Leah Tutu; Seated: Gloria Gaines, Thandi, Elizabeth Enloe

Leah Tutu Press Conference. Elizabeth Enloe, Jean Young, Leah Tutu, Thandi

Carol Luther During Leah Tutu Press Conference

All four photos: Terry Foss, AFSC Archives

Permission of AFSC Archives

Public address, Morehouse College

Permission of AFSC Archives

Left to right singing We Shall Overcome: Coretta Scott King, Elizabeth Enloe, Dr. Hugh M. Gloster (President, Morehouse College), Dean Lawrence E. Carter (Martin Luther King, Jr., International Chapel), Julian Bond, John Lewis, Alice Lovelace, two event co-sponsors

Terry Foss, AFSC Archives

Thandi Conversing with Police Escort in Jackson, MS

Permission of AFSC Archives

Manas Buthelezi–July 1986

Manas Buthelezi, Bishop of the Lutheran Church and President of the South African Council of Churches, visited Atlanta in 1986 as a guest of our Southern Africa Program, the Interdenominational Theological Center, and the Reverend Joseph Lowery and the SCLC. Our program arranged the press conference at Pascal's, and a potluck meal with discussion at which Bishop Buthelezi was unable to speak openly and frankly, given the State of Emergency in South Africa. This kind of repression strengthened our resolve to end apartheid.

Peter Magubane–1988

Augmenting our educational outreach, we sponsored a photography exhibit entitled "Facing South," held in Atlanta in 1988. Peter Magubane made available his photographs of Soweto 1976 to display in the company of Jim Alexander's images of African Americans struggling for dignity. Though Peter was unable to be in the US at the time of the exhibit, we held a reception in both his and Jim's honor and welcomed the public over a two-week period.

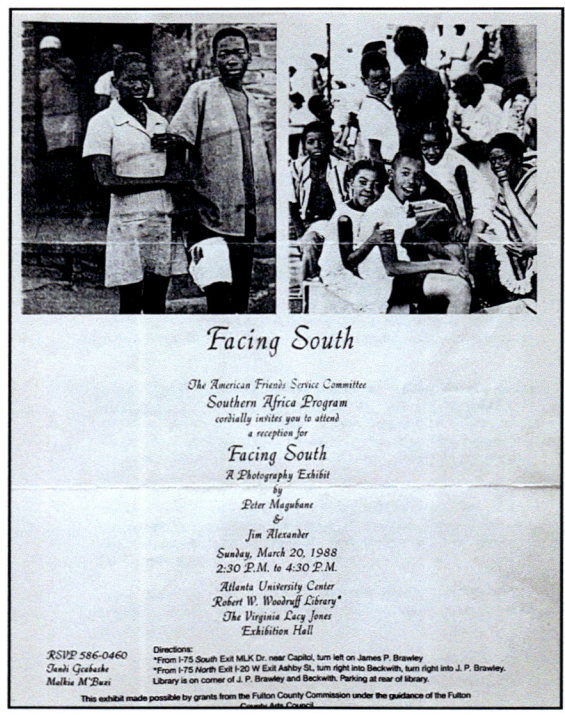

Permission of AFSC Archives

Dennis Brutus–1991

Dennis Brutus Speaking in Atlanta

Permission of AFSC Archives

Memorial:
Samora Moises Machel–AFSC offices, 1986

Organizing memorials were especially difficult and sad occasions:

> The death of Samora Machel, President of Mozambique, was a time of great sorrow for the Southern Africa Program. It is believed that the plane was shot down by the South African government while it was flying over South African territory. This action is particularly significant due to the current developments in the region…the front-line states were acting in concert against the South African government, and Samora Machel was returning from a strategy meeting at the time of his death.

I devoted myself to the planning committee for the memorial service held at the Interdenominational Theological Center Chapel on Friday, October 31 where Andrew Young, then mayor of Atlanta, delivered the eulogy.

Sister City Project–Braklaagte

By 1988, a new anti-apartheid strategy emerged which promoted the establishment of direct people-to-people links between US communities and South African communities threatened under apartheid in South Africa. The AFSC's US/South Africa Sister Community Project, chaired by Faye McDonald-Smith, worked with the Atlanta City Council to adopt a community under threat of forced removal and relocation. The program received information of increased beatings, detentions, closure of schools and clinics, and general harsh treatment of the citizens of Braklaagte who resisted their forced incorporation into the homeland of Bophutatswana.

The Project got a boost in 1989 when Mayor Andrew Young signed a City Council proclamation declaring Braklaagte a Sister Community to Atlanta.

By 1992, the program had exposed the Braklaagte situation to the citizens of Atlanta, conducted petition signing, letter writing, and telephoning campaigns to the US Ambassador to South Africa and the South African Ambassador to the United States, asking them to intervene on behalf of the people of Braklaagte and establish people-to-people contact between the two communities, with a special emphasis on churches and schools.

10

Cultural and Sports Boycotts

The International Cultural Boycott

The cultural boycotts of entertainers popularized the anti-apartheid movement in Atlanta and the southeast, raising awareness and preparing for the much harder task of explaining and encouraging economic sanctions and divestment. Forgoing a concert ticket felt a relatively benign act and far less complex a matter than financial divestment.

In 1958, in response to appeals from the African National Congress, the All African People's Conference in Accra called for an academic and cultural boycott of South Africa. By 1968, activists, prominent individuals, and international and professional organizations were demonstrating solidarity with the South African resistance. That year the United Nations General Assembly passed a resolution calling for sanctions against South Africa. In 1980 the General Assembly passed a resolution expressly calling on countries, intellectuals, artists, and athletes to honor an international boycott of cultural, academic, and sporting exchanges with South Africa.

Operationally, the cultural boycotts were facilitated by a continually updated United Nations *Register of Entertainers, Actors and Others Who Have Performed in Apartheid South Africa*. The first register named 211 individuals and groups who had performed knowingly or in opposition to the boycott. Maintained by the UN Centre Against Apartheid, as of 1983 the registry was a resource for us and for anti-apartheid groups worldwide. The consequence of one's name being on the list was to be confronted with demonstrations and pickets when performing.

> 1980: UN General Assembly Resolution 35/206 summary:
>
> The United Nations General Assembly makes the request to all states to prevent all cultural, academic, sporting, and other exchanges with South Africa. This is also an appeal to writers, artists, musicians, and other personalities to boycott South Africa. It urges all academic and cultural institutions to terminate all links with South Africa.

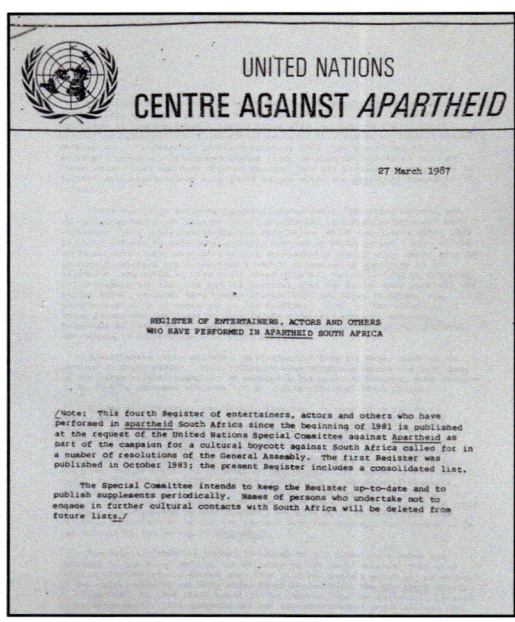

The Centre did recognize and delete the names of those entertainers who turned down invitations to perform in South Africa, canceled scheduled performances, or publicly indicated they would no longer perform in South Africa.

As a countermeasure, the South African regime offered exorbitant financial sums to performers in an attempt to defuse images of apartheid's realities and offset the country's growing isolation. Hosting celebrities such as Ray Charles, Millie Jackson, and Frank Sinatra were concerted attempts to cast South Africa in a positive light and promote a sophisticated image of the regime to the world.

The regime went so far as to confer non-white visitors the status of "honorary white" after a road accident involving a black star who was refused ambulance assistance when attendants discovered he was black. After a few such embarrassing occurrences the honorary status assured protection from suffering the degradation of being black.

Georgia Coalition volunteers monitored entertainers scheduled to perform in Atlanta, demonstrated at the performance sites, and advocated boycotts of those who had performed in South Africa in violation of the Cultural Boycott. Before a demonstration, our prerequisite was advance correspondence with the performer requesting to meet, and to explain how entertainers essentially demonstrated, intentionally or not, their support for the racist system by performing in South Africa. We requested their compliance, and, depending on their response, either called off or proceeded with the demonstration. We succeeded in some instances and in others we did not.

Boycotts and Pickets of Entertainers in Atlanta

I well remember our first boycott, in 1983. It was of the jazz performer, Chick Corea, at the Fox Theater. This demonstration put us on the national map of the Cultural Boycott. The Corea demonstration was followed by pickets and boycotts of other stars during the early to mid 1980s. Always it was poignant when we demonstrated before black stars who were willing to perform before primarily white-only audiences.

But we did it.

Cultural and Sports Boycotts

Frank Sinatra had sung at Sun City and we called attention to the resort's egregious nature during his concert at the Fox Theater on June 1, 1984. In an attempt to woo artists and performers from countries opposed to the apartheid system, the South African government permitted blacks and whites to meet socially at Sun City, where such encounters had previously been prohibited. Sun City lay one hour away from Johannesburg in one of the Bantustans, which the government promoted as quasi-independent states and the international community refused to recognize as such. Steven Van Zandt's 1985 song, *Ain't Gonna Play Sun City,* was recorded by "Artists United Against Apartheid" and helped popularize not only the egregious nature of Sun City but also the Cultural Boycott.

We boycotted other entertainers, such as Helen Reddy and Kenny Rogers. Friends remember a noisy protest at a Ray Charles Concert. Gloria Gaines and others of the Coalition spoke to Howard Hesseman and convinced him to speak publicly against future trips by entertainers to South Africa. He was very accommodating and did speak out as opposed to Ray Charles who refused to speak against concerts in South Africa.

The Reverend Isaac Miller and Volunteers at Fox Theater Protesting Frank Sinatra

Paul Simon Concert

Adherence to principles matters. This came poignantly into play with the Ladysmith Black Mambazo Paul Simon concert at the Omni in Atlanta on June 15, 1987. In this particular instance, the lines determining the violation of the Cultural Boycott were blurry. Simon made his highly creative, inspiring multi-Grammy winning album, *Graceland*, with the prominent South African musicians. They rehearsed in South Africa and recorded the performance at an outdoor stadium in Harare, Zimbabwe.

Thandi with Anti-Apartheid Volunteer

The controversy turned on whether Simon should be considered in violation of the UN boycott, given that he was providing opportunities to South African musicians, displaying their work, culture, and talent, and exposing them to international audiences.

The application of guiding principles demanded our careful evaluation and we concluded to stick with our boycott caveat of entertainers visiting South Africa. I was tormented by our decision to boycott, not because it was wrong; it wasn't wrong. But, as it did then, to this day it still aches me as my close colleagues, Miriam Makeba and Hugh Masekela, featured in the concert. And, it had won endorsement from Julian Bond who supported anti-apartheid initiatives.

Cultural Events We Supported

An interesting juxtaposition to the boycotted events were those performances we did promote, sponsor, and participate in. All movingly elicited the heart of the apartheid experience.

Jomandi Production of Athol Fugard's *Boseman and Lena* (26-27 October 1984)

You could substitute South Georgia for South Africa and the play would still be extremely applicable. Oppression breeds frustration and frustration breeds violence, and I've certainly seen a lot of that here in Georgia.

A. Reginald Eaves, Fulton County Commissioner

Asinamali! (1986)

The play, ***Asinamali!***, originating in South Africa, created by a South African playwright Mbongeni Ngema, and featuring South African performers and directors, was to be performed at the Academy Theatre. There was much debate among the Southern Africa staff and the Georgia Coalition members on whether we should boycott the play, demonstrate at the site, or attend it, given the play's sponsorship by the Coca-Cola Company. We decided to support the play despite its sponsors. *Asinamali!* was intense and far-reaching in its emotional impact.

My Soul Has Been Purified—a film of the life of Winne Mandela (February 22, 1987)

We joined with various partners—Atlanta African Film Society, Call to Conscience Network, GCDSA, Student Coalition Against Apartheid and Racism, and Student Government of Morehouse—to co-sponsor this event.

The International Sports Boycott

The Sports Boycott prohibited South African athletes from playing in foreign countries and foreign teams from playing in South Africa. Sports are extremely popular and emotive activities imbued with patriotism. As a result, the boycott proved to be hugely punishing for the South Africans. It was a success in Europe, Australia, New Zealand, and the Caribbean countries, which shared interests in soccer, rugby, and cricket. In the US, tennis and golf received appropriate attention from the anti-apartheid activists, but in the southern United States, not much happened in this arena.

1964:	International Olympic Committee withdraws South Africa's invitation to 1964 Olympic Games. Sporting boycotts begin.
1970:	International Olympic Committee withdraws recognition of South African Olympic Committee.
1981:	South African rugby tour of New Zealand last major tour as marred by protests.
1984:	United Nations Security Council urges member states to "restrict sporting contacts" with South Africa. The European Community adopts a similar code the following year.
1991:	African Olympic umbrella body recognizes the interim National Olympic Committee of South Africa (NOCSA). IOC offers provisional recognition to NOCSA and gives South Africa 180 days to remove apartheid laws and achieve nonracial controlling bodies for sports.

We supported as best we could the efforts of Artists and Athletes Against Apartheid, established in 1983 and co-chaired by Arthur Ashe and Harry Belafonte.

I was in good company with Joseph Lowery and Julian Bond when I wrote in March 1984 to Vince Dooley, the University of Georgia's head football coach and athletic director, who planned to travel to South Africa with the Georgia Bulldog Club, a loosely structured booster club:

> We would like the opportunity to discuss your plans for the upcoming tour. It is important that we fully understand your position and you understand us. We would like to meet with you as soon as possible. May I suggest early next week? Are you aware that any blacks who would accompany you on your tour of South Africa must be classified as "Honorary White" for them to travel without restriction with your group?

Vince Dooley eventually changed his mind, citing team unity, and I wrote (April 11, 1984) to commend him on his decision and to recommend he also postpone his proposed personal trip until apartheid was abolished.

Fundraiser for Georgia Coalition for Divestment in South Africa
Carol Luther and Gloria Gaines

Permission of Elizabeth Enloe

11

Divestment:

Federal and State Legislation, Economic Sanctions and Boycotts

Last Best Hope

The calls to end corporate investments in apartheid became the single, most important international effort to isolate the South Africa white regime and bring an end to apartheid. Without draconian economic isolation of South Africa, there would have been little incentive for the white minority to end the brutal apartheid laws.

I believed the withdrawal of financial support to be the last meaningful leverage to end apartheid nonviolently. Otherwise, the violence in my country would escalate.

US Investment in South Africa and Opposition to Divestment

Up until the early 1980s, absent any legislative restrictions or significant public pressure, over 125 US banks loaned billions of dollars to the South African government. US federal, state, and local governments were investing employees' pension funds and taxpayer dollars in South Africa. Close to 400 US corporations were in South Africa with subsidiaries or affiliates making profits and paying taxes to the South African government, and approximately 6,000 were present with licensing agreements. The South African economy was strong. The country's material wealth had attracted large numbers of multinationals over the previous decades.

Concerted opposition to divestment was strong and convincing to some. The South African government lobbied Congress and US business, maintaining that their internal problems were resolvable, and their investment standing was strong. There were invitations to US legislators to visit South Africa and warnings of million-dollar losses should divestment occur.

President Reagan and Constructive Engagement

While abhorrence of the increasingly visible apartheid atrocities was becoming almost universal outside South Africa, opposition to US divestment had its staunch defenders, most prominently the President of the United States. In direct contradiction to the international call for comprehensive sanctions and disinvestment, in the early 1980s Ronald Reagan elevated the concept of "constructive engagement" to US foreign policy. Proponents of constructive engagement promoted quiet diplomacy and continued US presence within the country. Not only was South Africa a major supplier of mineral wealth but it was a perceived ally against the specter of communism.

I was, of course, opposed to—and in my talks discredited—the policy of constructive engagement. It was false to claim that in lieu of a US withdrawal of support, US bank loans, trade, and business engagement would influence the gradual elimination of the apartheid laws. Instead, US investments in the billions of dollars continued to bestow credibility on South Africa. Investments furthered South Africa's economic expansion, including the ability to purchase military and police equipment to repress the expanding level of protest at home. The notion was ludicrous that the very presence of US companies would improve the employment status of black South Africans. Apartheid laws enforced blatant discrimination of the vast majority.

Divestment Movement Gains Strength

Incremental divestment achievements during the 1970s multiplied during the 1980s. Over years, through arduous efforts on many fronts, divestment campaigns raised awareness of the role that US corporations played in maintaining apartheid, and of how those corporations benefitted from that system. Similar campaigns were underway in Europe and worldwide. In its various manifestations, divestment called on corporations, states, financial institutions, municipalities, universities, and individual professionals to cut ties with the South African government and economy.

The financial business world—the banks, pension funds, and insurance companies—that provided apartheid's lifeline in the form of capital and loans to South Africa were pressured by legislation and the anti-apartheid movement. Resistant US federal, state, and local governments as well as corporations, and institutions felt increased pressures as conditions in South Africa deteriorated and the anti-apartheid movement strengthened. Corporations that had embraced the *Sullivan Principles* faced challenges to divest from their constituents and from the public at large.

US Federal Legislation—Comprehensive Anti-Apartheid Act (CAAA), 1986

The bills that were to become the Comprehensive Anti-Apartheid Act were making their way through both houses of the US Congress in the early 1980s. Both the House and Senate versions had had a long lifespan since the first formal presentation by Ronald Dellums, a black Congressman from California, in 1972. Two versions of the bill were finally reintroduced for debate, negotiation, and compromise in 1985 and favorably won passage in 1986 with wide and strong bi-partisan support. This was a remarkable achievement for a Democrat-controlled House of Representatives and a Republican majority in the Senate. Essentially, the Act enacted multiple sanctions against South Africa as a means to bring an end to apartheid.

Most, though not all, US legislators held positions distinct from President Reagan's constructive engagement. Reagan called the bill "economic warfare" and, I need to say, that's precisely what it was. He lived up to his threat to veto the bill, but in a rare event on a matter of international foreign policy the US Congress overrode the veto, and the Comprehensive Anti-Apartheid Act went into effect, further isolating the apartheid government.

To put it mildly, we at the AFSC and GCDSA, along with many others, were pleased. By no means can our efforts—speeches explaining the bill's importance, urging individuals to contact their elected representatives, distribution of thousands of ACOA's brochure, *Voices for Withdrawal*—be described as extensive or as having a direct impact, but we were glad to have led a regional effort of support. We were not discouraged by President Reagan's continued commitment to constructive engagement. The voices demanding an end to this "crime against humanity" were being heard. Our public education and advocacy continued as subsequent Congressional sanctions bills were put forward.

Pressing Forward

We prepared ourselves to navigate encounters with audiences from individuals to corporations who opposed divestment. Our political, economic, and moral arguments developed strength. Visceral experiences, whether from a film or performance or personal encounters with someone victimized by apartheid, inevitably illuminated the moral underpinnings of our position. We committed ourselves to address effectively those audiences holding views different than our own, practiced what to expect, and became more strategic.

One practice session occurred during a long evening meeting at the AFSC offices in 1985 when we challenged ourselves to list and discuss twenty reasons for and against divestment. "US corporations promote social change" was paired with "Wrong to profit from apartheid." Bill Withers, a member of the Georgia Coalition and resident of Quaker House, led us through a warm-up exercise in which we physically divided ourselves into two groups: those representing black South Africans found themselves relegated to one-quarter of the conference room while the four persons representing all other races freely walked throughout the entire span of offices.

Atlanta City Council and Georgia State Legislature

Julian Bond, then a Georgia State Senator, had laid bare the task before legislators in his keynote address to 200 state and municipal legislators at the National Conference on Public Investment and South Africa in June of 1981 in New York City:

> We are here, then, to force the disengagement of our commonly held wealth from this evil. I think we all realize that this will be a difficult and time-consuming process, for we are in effect opposing the whole of American history. The current condition of American black people, political and economic, is more than well known. We gather here to ask the U.S. to honor the principle that no person's worth is superior to another, to do in foreign affairs what is yet to be done at home.

The AFSC and the Georgia Coalition increased awareness and mobilized constituent support throughout the state for divestment legislation. We initiated letter-writing campaigns to the governor and legislative members and organized educational forums, news conferences, and public hearings. We provided testimony; Mack Jones testified in February 1985 before the Georgia General Assembly on behalf of the Georgia Coalition.

Preparing for Testimony before Georgia General Assembly
Malkia M'Buzi Moore, Diane Mattewitz, Brian Spears, Thandi, unidentified man, the Reverend Timothy McDonald

Permission of Elizabeth Enloe

Divestment

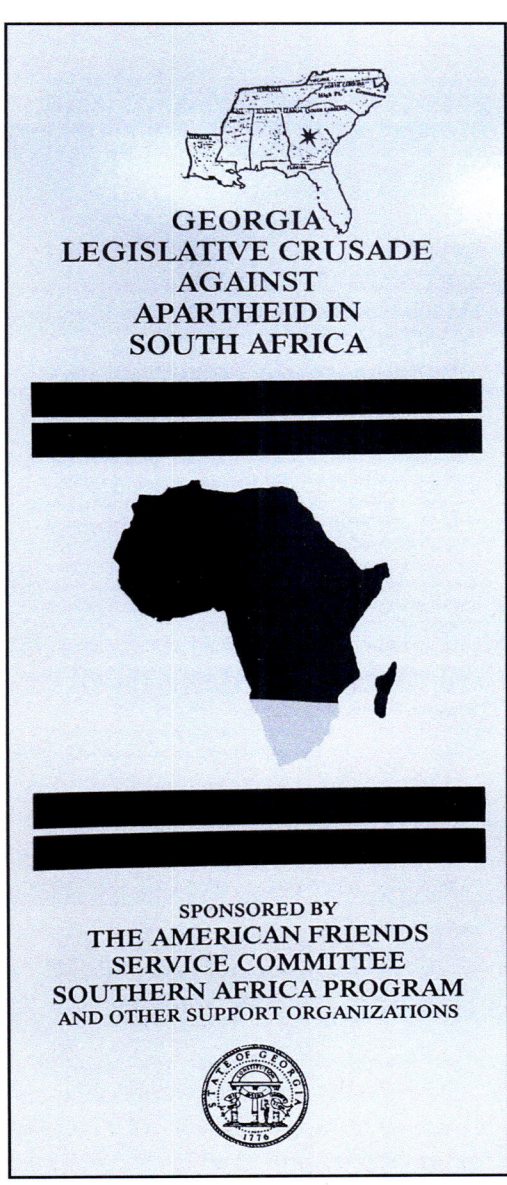

Permission of AFSC Archives

Our Legislative Crusade Against Apartheid aimed at extending these efforts throughout the state not only to Atlanta, but also to Macon, Albany, Columbus, Savannah, Augusta, Athens, and Rome.

True to our commitment to partner with other organizations, we were joined in these efforts by the Georgia Association of Educators, Atlanta Federation of Teachers, Atlanta Friends Meeting, Vietnam Veterans Against the War, the National Lawyers Guild, and others.

Atlanta's City Council did vote affirmatively to prohibit new investments of employee pension funds in companies doing business in South Africa.

At the State level matters were less successful.

We worked closely over many years with Tyrone Brooks, a former field representative of the Southern Christian Leadership Conference and a Georgia State Representative and Chairman of the Georgia Legislative Black Caucus.

On April 15, 1983, Tyrone Brooks addressed the United Nations Special Committee Against Apartheid. He announced his intent to introduce the following year to the Georgia General Assembly legislation to prohibit investment of public monies, primarily retirement pension funds, in banks doing business with or operating in or dealing with South Africa. Legislators Betty J. Clark and J.C. Daugherty, Mary Young-Cummings, Mabel Thomas, Sanford Bishop, and other legislators in the Georgia Legislature also embraced the issue and supported the South African struggle without hesitation. I suspect that, as black legislators in the South, they felt a visceral connection to the South African struggle.

Neither Julian nor Tyrone succeeded in convincing a majority of state legislators, who voted in opposition of divestment in 1984, 1985, 1986, and every

Left to right: Malkia M'Buzi Moore, Tyrone Brooks, Margaret Roach, Thandi
AFSC Offices

Permission of Elizabeth Enloe

year thereafter. The legislators of the Georgia Assembly never joined the mounting number of states passing divestment legislation.

Nonetheless, Tyrone Brooks never ceased to introduce the bills annually. Every year he passionately asked the State of Georgia to divest. Every year the legislators voted "No."

Colleges and Universities

The role of US college and university students in the anti-apartheid movement cannot be overstated. Heightened activism on campuses increased public awareness. Johns Hopkins was a divestment leader among the universities, as were Ohio University, Hampshire College, and the University of Massachusetts—all of which had divested by 1982. ACOA tracked divestment actions by educational institution. There were 53 divested universities in total in 1984. The unrelenting campaigns by students resulted in a total of 155 US universities divesting by 1988.

In Atlanta we supported student efforts on the various campuses. The two-year effort of the Georgia State University Student Coalition Against Apartheid and Racism, chaired by Dwayne Redding, influenced the December 10, 1986, vote by the Georgia Board of Regents to divest their stocks and securities portfolio.

We spoke often on the Morehouse College campus. The August 1985 event drew over 2,000 students as I joined Andrew Young, Julian Bond, and John Lewis on the

Meeting with Spelman Board of Directors: Unidentified man, Thandi Gcabashe, Marian Wright Edelman (Chair of the Spelman Board of Trustees), an unidentified man, Andrew Young

podium with Mpho Tutu and Bernice King, all three of us daughters of Nobel Peace Prize winners.

So, too, Spelman College students lent their support throughout the years. There was cause for celebration upon the April 1986 vote to divest by the Board of Trustees. During the weekend before the Board's decision, several of us including myself and Andrew Young met with members of the Board. I was quoted as having said, "Do you really tell me that you are going to be educated with the blood money of your own black brothers and sisters of South Africa? I have a hard time believing that." That sounds to be a fairly accurate quote of my position.

With time we were able to take credit in the disinvestment of nine universities in the South.

Daughters of Nobel Peace Prize Laureates: Mpho Tutu (daughter of Leah and Desmond Tutu), Thandi, Bernice King (daughter of Coretta and Martin Luther King), with Able Mable Thomas (Georgia State Representative)

Atlanta University Student Anti-Apartheid Prayer Vigil and Protest, King Chapel, Morehouse College

Permission of Susan J. Ross

Bank Loans

The AFSC national office began divestment dialogues with Chase Manhattan Bank in 1965 and in 1969 withdrew its funds and closed its account in protest of Chase's continued loans to South Africa. Our work with banks in Atlanta was modest, though the Georgia Coalition's research identified C&S Bank, First National Bank, and Trust Company Bank as among the biggest Atlanta lenders. My predecessor, Herbert Katedza, began outreach in 1979, writing to Atlanta banks, requesting that they state their respective positions. The Trust Company Bank's December 12, 1979 response indicated they had "no involvement whatsoever in South Africa." The December 17, 1979 letter from Citizens and Southern National Bank indicated it "would be inappropriate to discuss relations with any third party."

Anti-Apartheid Demonstration outside First National Bank, Atlanta
Alice Lovelace and Jon Michael

Permission of Alice Lovelace

Demonstrations at Corporate Offices in Atlanta

We disseminated information to individuals as taxpayers and consumers of corporate products, and as persons who knowingly or unknowingly had pension funds, stocks, bonds, or equities in companies with investments in South Africa. We offered an understanding of how this was a collusion with apartheid. Ultimately, individuals were encouraged to withdraw their business from South Africa–related companies and banks, and those entities were urged to divest themselves from South Africa.

Much as we depended upon the UN for Cultural Boycott updates, we similarly reviewed reports on US corporate investments and stances from the national anti-apartheid organizations such as ACOA, Interfaith Center for Corporate Responsibility, and Campaign to Oppose Bank Loans to South Africa. Among the various news reports and sources flowing into the office, ACOA's "Unified List" periodically compiled and updated the firms with investments, loans, or licensing/franchising agreements in South Africa and Namibia. The status of companies changed, and we remained current as we organized demonstrations before Atlanta-based firms. In 1985 we initiated a series of on-site demonstrations against Atlanta-based companies.

Of particular interest to us were those firms with home offices in Georgia—The Coca-Cola Company and Royal Crown Company in Atlanta, and West Point-Pepperell, Inc. in West Point, Georgia. Also of interest were those corporate investors with regional offices in Atlanta: Burroughs Corporation, Control Data Corporation, Firestone Tire and Rubber, Ford Motor Company, General Electric Company, Goodyear Tire and Rubber, IBM, Mobil Oil, and National Cash Register.

Of the top 20 US investors in South Africa, five had headquarters or regional offices in Atlanta: Coca-Cola, Ford, General Electric, General Motors, and IBM.

We were not alone in Atlanta in undertaking this work. SCLC challenged the Southern Company, based in Biloxi, Mississippi, for its importation of South African coal and successfully boycotted the Winn Dixie grocery store chain to cease its sale of South African can fruits and frozen fish products.

The Georgia Coalition encouraged the Atlanta-based M&M Products Company to end ties with South Africa. M&M Products, Incorporated, was a black-owned hair care company and was, in 1985, the 11th largest black-owned company in the United States. The company initially claimed that they were not directly involved in the country but that their products were merely being distributed there. That was a difference without a distinction.

In a reversal of position, M&M agreed to divest:

> While the Company stands to suffer financial setbacks in its international sales as a result of this action, M&M feels that is in keeping with its concerns and those of the Black community world-wide to disassociate itself from Vivid Distributors… M&M has taken the step … in order to end the perception that M&M's relationship is inconsistent with it[s] stand against the reprehensible system of apartheid in South Africa.

Perhaps the first high-profile demonstrations took place outside the Georgia Stamp and Coin Shop in downtown Atlanta. In our educational outreach to the public, we tied the coin shop's sale of the Krugerrand to the brutal economic exploitation of South African gold miners—the dangerous working conditions, high mortality, poor payment, and separation from family. These connections quickly caught peoples' attention.

Approximately 120 to 130 people participated in the demonstration before the headquarters of Coca-Cola on March 27th, 1985. Though we were unclear about the mayor's position, we were advised in advance that the pending demonstration displeased Coca-Cola officials, who called SCLC and the King Center leadership, suggesting they not participate. Leaders and staff of those organizations were not present at the demonstration, signaling to us of the work ahead with key members of Atlanta's black community. At the demonstration, Mack Jones spoke to the protestors and, after thanking them for attending, said, "The fact that Coca-Cola did everything it could to prevent people from coming… shows that no one person or group can control anybody. When the people speak, people with money tremble."

At the General Motors Lakewood Plant on the corner of Sawtell and McDonough across from the Atlanta Federal Penitentiary, the GCDSA sponsored a demonstration on April 10, 1985. GM was one of the ten largest US corporations invested in South Africa and it addressed one of the country's three major strategic needs—automobiles. It was the largest employer of black South Africans. Its plant was documented to have been built to convert to military equipment production within 48 hours.

We picketed the IBM shareholders annual meeting at the Civic Center later that month, on April 19th, 1985. Atlanta police met us at the bottom of the steps leading up to the Center, indicating we'd be arrested if we crossed a specific line. Several of us crossed the line, and several of us including John Lewis, Tyrone Brooks, and Mack Jones were arrested. I, too, crossed the line and was arrested and it did shake me up a bit. Gloria Gaines was asked to stay behind as we stepped forward to be arrested. Her duty was to collect us from the police station. Charges were dropped on April 30.

IBM supplied and serviced computers for government agencies. Dissident employees and shareholders employed shareholder resolutions, pickets, internal organizing, and news conferences to bring IBM's role to light. They even produced a campaign button saying, "IBM Computes Apartheid."

IBM followed a familiar script: seeming to comply while changing nothing. IBM announced that it was selling its South African business, but apart from the name ("IBM" became "ISM"), nothing changed. They sold their equity in the South African subsidiary but continued to supply technology, technical assistance, and servicing through ISM.

We joined in the Royal Dutch Shell Boycott and carried Shell Boycott materials to our speaking engagements, answering questions as they arose. Due to demands on or staff and volunteers, we were unable to give this boycott the attention it deserved.

Shell supplied fuel for the South Africa military and police and was considered a strategic supplier, since it was the country's major source of fuel. It also operated a coal mine where laborers were coerced to work, which was the proximate cause for the boycott. The call came from South Africa's National Union of Mineworkers, the nation's largest black union.

That call was raised in the United States by the Free South Africa Movement and the United Mine Workers Union. It went to local anti-apartheid activists on campuses and throughout the country. It was answered by activists countrywide, by the World Council of Churches, major religious organizations, by the AFL-CIO, the NAACP, the National Organization for Women, and, from abroad, the International Confederation of Free Trade Unions, as well as student organizations, and a wide range of citizens' groups.

Sullivan Principles

Rather than leave South Africa, American corporations jumped at the chance to comply with the *Sullivan Principles* or at least to attempt to comply. Authored and promoted by the Reverend Leon Sullivan in 1977, the *Principles* were a code of conduct (or set of standards) focused on equality of treatment of black laborers working for US corporations in South Africa. They called for companies to implement non-segregation in the work setting, fair employment practices, job training, and advancement. Sullivan maintained that US corporations could achieve reform from within the country.

An active black minister of a large congregation in Philadelphia, and member of the board of General Motors, Leon Sullivan attracted almost half of the 300-plus US companies with businesses in South Africa. They became signatories and agreed in principle to institute the codes. Compliance was to be rated through a survey by an independent firm, Arthur D. Little, Co.

Permission of Elizabeth Schmidt

From the outset, the anti-apartheid movement in the US largely rejected the *Sullivan Principles* as a ploy to appease without protesting the fundamental and structural evils of the system. Corporations by their limited engagement might have positive impact within their workplace over which they had some control, but not with respect to the condition for millions of workers laboring under apartheid's laws.

Sullivan's *Principles* were an impediment to sanctions and divestment. We had our share of explaining the principles. They muddied the waters and required us to expend huge energies in the explanation of their faults. The early 1980s analysis by Elizabeth Schmidt substantiated claims of their ineffectiveness in the larger context of apartheid. In the mid-1980s, Sullivan himself abandoned the support of his own principles, as they had not led to the demise of apartheid.

The Coca-Cola Company was a signatory to the *Sullivan Principles*. Coca-Cola was one of the corporations that remained in South Africa, with the *Principles* as one premise for doing so.

Divestment Guidelines Updated in Wake of Corporate Divestments Announcements

As major corporations in rapid succession in the mid-1980s announced their intent to divest, we gave a hard look at what each company claimed constituted divestment and what they actually proposed to do. Some resorted to indirect investments to get around the international boycott, but others divested outright. The financial transfers and apparent indirect investments of some corporations gave us reason to investigate. Staff of the major US anti-apartheid organizations convened in late 1986 in the immediate wake of divestment announcements by IBM, GM, and Coca-Cola and issued in January 1987 a set of refined and definitive guidelines of what constituted divestment:

> …an increasing number of U.S. companies have moved to end their direct investment in South Africa. However, many of these companies are not really pulling out. …it is essential to distinguish between those corporations for which withdrawal means the termination of all economic ties to South Africa, and those for which withdrawal merely indicates a restructuring of economic relations.

Guidelines for Divestment

We support an end to all corporate involvement in or with South Africa and Namibia. A corporation is doing business in or with the Republic of South Africa or Namibia if it, its parent, or its subsidiaries:

1. have direct investments in South Africa or Namibia, or have entered into franchise, licensing, or management agreements with or for any entity in those countries; or
2. are financial institutions that have not prohibited new investments, loans, credits or related services, or the renewal of existing financial agreements, including those for the purpose of trade, with any entity in those countries; or
3. have more … [than] 5% of their common stock beneficially owned or controlled by a South African entity.

A company with operations in South Africa or Namibia for the sole purpose of reporting the news shall not be considered doing business in those countries.

American Committee on Africa (ACOA),
American Friends Service Committee (AFSC),
Interfaith Center for Corporate Responsibility (ICCR),
TransAfrica,
Washington Office on Africa (WOA)

IBM, General Motors, and Coca-Cola were listed as not having fully withdrawn their investments. With these simple and unequivocal criteria, we were well placed to launch a national boycott of Coca-Cola.

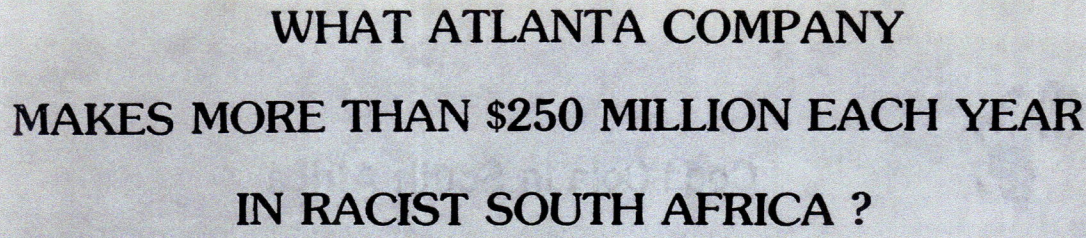

12

Coca-Cola Divestment *Campaign* and Coca-Cola *Boycott*

Overview Overview of the *Campaign*

From the beginning, The Coca-Cola Company was one of several companies in our corporate divestment focus. It was among the top twenty US corporate investors in South Africa. Coca-Cola's international headquarters was a short distance from our AFSC office. Appeals to divest and then demonstrations at the corporate headquarters began in the mid-1980s.

Coke's History in South Africa

entered South African market 1938
48 years of profits during entrenchment of apartheid laws
dominant name in the South African soft industry
with 69% of the market
one of largest American employers in S.A.
4,765 employees (IRRC 1985)
1985 worldwide sales of $7.9B and $1.05B profits
~$50M estimated for sale of syrup to S.A. bottlers
S.A. 1985 sales account for 5% of total sales

Assets/Ownership

30% of the shares in the bottling company
55% of the shares of the canning corporation
sole owner of the syrup concentrate plant

Atlanta Journal/Constitution, 9/17/86;
NY Times, 9/17/86; ICCR, 1985

The Divestment *Campaign* had its conceptual beginnings in 1981 and its concrete plans by 1984. It was a project of the influential and all-volunteer (except for me) Georgia Coalition for Divestment in South Africa which organized the initial demonstrations. AFSC was the *Campaign*'s co-sponsor. The endorsement of over 50 national, state, and local organizations ensured the grassroots essence of the *Campaign* over the nine years of its duration.

Despite its stated abhorrence of apartheid, Coca-Cola, a signatory to the *Sullivan Principles*, established its solution to the mounting pressure for disinvestment and remained steadfast in its position. Coca-Cola had resources to orchestrate in 1986 both a withdrawal of assets and a retention of a market in South Africa.

We contested the scope of disinvestment. After many efforts on our part and that of others to urge a complete disinvestment, the *Campaign* eventually escalated to a boycott.

This was the one and only national initiative in the United States launched from the Atlanta office. Our work was limited financially, but we had clarity, commitment, and staying power. The *Campaign* captured the imagination of young people throughout the country.

We did have our critics and detractors; painfully some were friends and colleagues in the anti-apartheid movement, both in Atlanta and South Africa. Influential reasons close to home involved the long association with Coca-Cola philanthropy. Through it all we maintained cordiality. Our focus was Coke, not individuals with whom we held differences.

In the early 1990s, when the anti-apartheid movement could see an end to the long struggle, we kept our sights on the fact that Nelson Mandela could not vote. Against prevailing winds, we urged the continued support for divestment until three years later when Mandela himself declared before the UN General Assembly on September 23, 1993 that South Africa was in a position for the international community to end economic sanctions.

Campaign Beginnings

The germ of the idea to focus on one company emerged during an evening conversation in 1981 after a long day of speaking engagements in the southeast US by anti-apartheid activists. Our respective organizations had taken seriously the call to divest and were avidly applying pressure on corporations. We were prepared to promote divestment, to support sanctions, and to undertake boycotts if needed. However, we could not effectively focus on all 300-plus US companies then invested in South Africa. To be pragmatic, we had to zero in on one.

Initially, Coca-Cola was one company along with IBM, General Motors, Holiday Inn, and others that we encouraged to divest through correspondence and demonstrations in 1985, 1986, and 1987. We learned that Coca-Cola was concerned enough about the demonstrations to call upon black leadership, urging that they refrain from participation.

Coca-Cola Divestment Campaign and Boycott Timeline	
Sept 1938:	Coca-Cola enters South Africa market
Fall 1981:	Conceptual beginnings of a campaign by anti-apartheid organizations
June 1985:	Georgia Coalition sponsors demonstrations at Coca-Cola Atlanta headquarters
Sept 1985:	Georgia Coalition announces Coca-Cola Divestment Campaign
Feb 26, 1986:	Coalition, AFSC, and Coca-Cola begin dialogues
March 1996:	Coca-Cola announces $10M Equal Opportunity Fund
Aug 21, 1986:	Coca-Cola announces it will remain in South Africa
Aug 1986:	Georgia Coalition announces intent to launch Boycott on Oct. 10, 1986
Sept 17, 1986:	Coca-Cola announces decision to divest
Sept 18, 1986:	Georgia Coalition and AFSC respond to Coca-Cola with press conference
Nov 8, 1986:	National anti-apartheid organizations issue explicit divestment criteria citing incomplete withdrawal by IBM, General Motors, and Coca-Cola
Dec 15, 1986:	Fact-Finding Team members and Coca-Cola officials meet
Dec 16, 1986:	Fact-Finding Team concludes Coca-Cola has not met divestment criteria
April 24, 1986:	Boycott of Coca-Cola products announced
Sept 15, 1989:	Bishop Tutu's letter widely circulated by Coca-Cola
Feb 10, 1990:	Nelson Mandela released from imprisonment
June 1990:	ANC turns down Coca-Cola's offer of assistance for Mandela's Atlanta visit
July 15, 1990:	Nelson Mandela at UN asks sanctions be reimposed
Early 1990s:	Georgia Coalition and AFSC urge continuation of sanctions and Boycott
July 1993:	AFSC formally concludes Campaign in anticipation of South Africa leadership request
Sept 25, 1993:	Nelson Mandela in UN General Assembly calls for end of sanctions

Why Coca-Cola?

Our research and planning over several years helped finalize the decision to "zero in on" Coca-Cola. While Coke had a uniquely positive image in the United States for its beverages and its financial support of institutions both public and private, still, it was making profits in South Africa and paying corporate taxes to the apartheid regime. They had embraced and continued to lean on the discredited *Sullivan Principles* to guide their presence. We were prepared to expose the contradiction between philanthropy in the US and support of a repressive regime abroad.

> As a major U.S. firm with very high name recognition and as a firm which has distinguished itself through its highly visible support for public and private institutions, and causes, the Coca-Cola Company is uniquely situated to show leadership to the business community of the U.S.A. and of the world. The Coca-Cola Company was selected for particular focus due to its number of assets in South Africa, its worldwide visibility, accessibility, and affordability as a consumer product to people of all economic classes.
>
> A History of the Coca-Cola *Boycott Campaign*

We believed Coca-Cola could be encouraged to take a major leadership role in divestment. A comprehensive and full divestment by Coke would set an impressive precedent and a distinctive model for other corporations to do likewise.

The *Campaign* Launch

Malkia M'Buzi Moore, Kuhusu Wanzu, Gloria Gaines, unidentified man, AFSC volunteer, Jon Michael, Thandi and AFSC volunteer in front of AFSC Atlanta Offices

Permission of Elizabeth Enloe

In September 1985, the Georgia Coalition announced The Coca-Cola Divestment *Campaign* to urge the Corporation's total economic disengagement from South Africa.

The *Campaign* was an invitation to Coke leadership "to do the right thing." We banked upon the facts to lead Coke's corporate decision makers to complete a full divestment and radical change in their dealings with the government of South Africa. We believed they would want to defend their image before a world now awakened to apartheid atrocities and divest.

From the September 1985 announcement and well into 1986, the Georgia Coalition and AFSC together laid the groundwork for a successful multi-tiered, national *Campaign*. We produced educational and promotional materials and mapped out *Campaign* governance between the Coalition and AFSC.

Endorsers

The success of the *Campaign*—a grassroots campaign—depended upon the engagement of national, regional, and local endorsers. Our first endorser was International Council of African Women. These organizations promoted the *Campaign* with their constituents in their local communities and nationally. They organized letter writing, hosted speakers, released press advisories, distributed fact sheets. Later, many became active in the *boycott*.

Campaign **Endorsers** (partial list)	**Co-Sponsor: American Friends Service Committee Endorsers:** ACTWU – Southern Region, Adrian Dominican Sisters 1989 – Adrian, MI, All Peoples Congress, Amalgamated Clothing and Textile Workers Union – Southeast Region, American Committee on Africa, American Federation of State, County, and Municipal Employees (AFSCME) – Atlanta, GA Local 144, American Postal Workers Union and Municipal Employees – 1986, Arizona Coalition Against Apartheid, Atlanta Committee on Latin America – 1986, Black Organizers Conference, Black Student Organization for Communication, University of Illinois – 1986, Boeing Aircraft, black employees – Seattle, Washington (1990 CC *Campaign* Newsletter), Black Vanguard Resource Center – Virginia, Capital District Coalition Against Apartheid and Racism, Casa Maria Community – Milwaukee, WI, Colorado Coalition Against Apartheid, Commission for Justice of the Sisters of Saint Joseph – 1991 – Philadelphia, Creative Peace Movement – CMU, Fellowship of Reconciliation, Florida State University (FSU) South Anti-Apartheid Committee (S.A.A.C) 1986, Florida State University Student Anti-Apartheid Committee, Georgia Citizen's Coalition on Hunger, International Council of African Women – Washington, D.C, International Council of Black Organizers, KMT Fraternity, Morehouse College – 1989, Mid-West Students Against Apartheid and Racism, National Black United Front – Chicago, National Lawyers Guild – Atlanta, National Nuclear Freeze Campaign, National U.S. Out of South Africa Network – New York, New Afrikan People's Organization, New York South Africa Boycott Committee (SABOL-NY), Nuclear Freeze/Jobs with Peace – Atlanta, Patrice Lumumba Coalition endorsed April 25, 1987, SAOC – New York, Southern Africa Liberation Committee – Michigan State University, Southern Africa Liberation Committee, Michigan State University, Michigan – 1986, Southern Students Conference Against Apartheid, Student Coalition Against Apartheid and Racism – (SCAAR) Georgia State University students, U.S. Out of Southern Africa Network/APC-PAM National Office, War Resisters League – Southeast, Washington Federation of State Employees, Local 1488, American Federation of State, County, Washington Office on Africa, Women for Racial and Economic Equality – Pittsburgh, PA, Women Outside for Women Inside

The *Campaign* stayed equally close to those who were unable to formally endorse but were willing to actively support. For example, the Interfaith Center for Corporate Responsibility wrote indicating the challenge of securing their full constituency of multiple religious denominations, as each would necessarily go through its organizational processes to agree on a boycott.

We anticipated resistance from some key Atlanta individuals and civil rights organizations, with whom we had worked for years and requested personal meetings to discuss our objectives and campaign developments. Some endorsed and some did not. We remained in contact to answer questions and offer updates.

We wrote to key individuals in South Africa—to Bishop Tutu, and to Allan Boesak, founder in 1983 of the of the United Democratic Front which consolidated hundreds of organizations and, with the ANC banned, played a central role of anti-apartheid organizing within South Africa. Letters also went to Winnie Mandela and the newly formed Congress of South Africa Trade Unions (COSATU), requesting their endorsement.

Dialogues with Coca-Cola

Essential to the *Campaign* were our dialogues and negotiations with Coca-Cola. The first meeting to share our perspectives took place on February 26, 1986, with Vice President Carl Ware and Brant Davis. I participated along with Ted Brodeck and Elizabeth Enloe. Coca-Cola President, Donald Keough, upon our request for a meeting, chose written communications.

It was largely Carl Ware with whom we talked throughout the years. He was, in 1982, Vice President of Urban Affairs and by 1986 had become Senior Vice President. Meetings, correspondence, phone calls continued throughout the *Campaign* into the early 1990s, principally between Carl Ware and me. He and I were, occasionally, guest speakers together on the same platform to speak about Coca-Cola and South Africa.

We found during and after the initial discussions in February 1986 that Coke was resistant to pull out its stake and assets from South Africa. They clarified their two-prong approach: first, doing business for profit; and second, assisting in ending apartheid. They brought forth arguments and reasons, including their compliance with the *Sullivan Principles*, and for some time deflected criticism of their presence in South Africa. Worth mentioning is that less than a year before, in May of 1985, Leon Sullivan himself acknowledged that the *Principles* were insufficient and that he would, within a specific time, support "withdrawal of all America companies in South Africa and a total economic embargo."

Coca-Cola's Economic Opportunity Fund (EOF)

In late March 1986, Coca-Cola announced the establishment of the Equal Opportunity Fund and Coke's commitment of $10M to support "programs in education, housing, and business development and related fields for black South Africans." The Fund's announcement was widely circulated, including to members of the US Congress. Success in attracting as trustees Allan Boesak and Desmond Tutu and other highly regarded black South Africans, with prominent roles in the anti-apartheid movement, was strategically used to offset criticism of their less-than-complete disinvestment. This action presented a major development with which the *Campaign* contended for years to come.

Decision to Boycott

Direct word from Coca-Cola in August 1986, almost a year after formally launching the *Campaign*, confirmed to us that Coke would not further pursue divestment. Coke would remain in South Africa. It was a moment of decision—escalate into a boycott, or not.

Consultation with *Campaign* endorsers found support for a boycott.

The Georgia Coalition members announced the decision to launch the *Boycott* of Coca-Cola products in two months' time, on October 10, 1986, during the observance of South African Prisoners Day.

Taken by Surprise, Coke's Divestment Announcement

Unanticipated and unexpectedly, on September 17, 1986, without word to us or advance public notice, and less than a month before our intended boycott announcement, Coca-Cola Company announced its decision to divest. It planned to sell all off its assets in South Africa as "a statement of our opposition to apartheid and of our support for the economic aspirations of Black South Africans." The company refuted speculations that it had responded to pressure by anti-apartheid organizations.

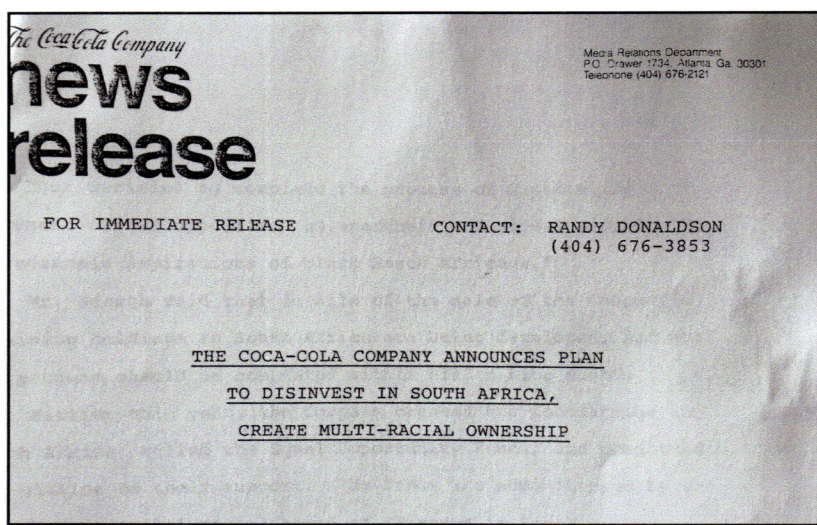

Atlanta, September 17, 1986 – The Coca-Cola Company News Release

The Coca-Cola Company Announces Plan to Disinvest in South Africa, Create Multi-Racial Ownership.

"We have been reducing our investment in South Africa since 1976, and we have now decided to sell our remaining holdings in the country," says Donald R. Keough, president and chief operating officer of The Coca-Cola Company.

"Our objective is not solely to disinvest, however. We will disinvest in a way that creates significant, multi-racial equity participation in the South African soft drink industry. Our goal is to structure the transactions in a way that improves the prospects of black South Africans and increases their ability to invest in their country's economy.

"Our decision to complete the process of disinvestment is a statement of our opposition to apartheid and of our support for the economic aspirations of black South Africans."

Our Response to Coca-Cola's Announcement

The following day, September 18, we hosted a news conference at the AFSC offices, attended by one news station only. Our statement contained questions focused on the motive, nature, and impact of Coke's action. With no time to digest the plan's details, it was all we could do in the moment, except to say, unequivocally, that, "There can be no reform of apartheid. Total disinvestment by Coca-Cola or any other foreign company must mean the cessation of all economic operations and connections, including license, trademarks, factories, suppliers, and distributors."

I spoke by phone with Carl Ware and offered to meet. He was not happy with our position.

In contrast to our response, praise for Coca-Cola was immediately forthcoming from Atlanta's mayor, Andrew Young, and from editorial writers of the city's major

AFSC's Moriba Karamoko with reporter
Permission of Elizabeth Enloe

newspapers, *The Atlanta Journal and Constitution* and the *Atlanta Inquirer*. Major national papers reported Coke's divestment.

It was a deep disappointment to me that the pastor of my church, Joseph Lowery, who had been among the prominent individuals to urge Coke to divest, praised Coke's plan. (SCLC had just completed a successful campaign, in 1986, urging Winn-Dixie to remove from its shelves South African products.) Dr. Lowery acknowledged pressure from other anti-apartheid groups to boycott and attributed SCLC's reluctance to Coca-Cola's "history of social responsibility' to the black community." Gloria and I wrote Dr. Lowery expressing our regret.

We suspended the imminent call for a boycott to determine the facts and to assess the impact of Coke's decision and whether Coke met the criteria for disinvestment, or not. I admit there was skepticism about the divestment plan.

We contacted *Campaign* endorsers, seeking their input. Reactions varied: was there a victory or not? There was confusion. Overall, endorsers requested information and direction.

The meeting of endorsers described earlier took place on November 8th in Philadelphia to unite on strategy. Together with the four other major US anti-apartheid organizations—American Committee on Africa, Interfaith Center on Corporate Responsibility, TransAfrica, and Washington Office on Africa—we drafted explicit, new guidelines for divestment.

With care and caution we proceeded, acting on sound advice not to pass premature judgement on Coke's action, and to reach out to those with whom we worked and with whom we shared a fundamental commitment to the end of apartheid, even though they supported Coke's plan.

We explained our campaign purpose and our assessment to our friends both in the United States and in South Africa. We made our questions to Coke publicly well-known. Elizabeth Enloe, my AFSC supervisor, was particular about going through the process of discovery, dialogue, and negotiation before declaring a boycott. Fortunately, her stance in this respect coincided with mine.

We attempted to determine what middle management felt about Coke's status in South Africa. There was contact with two key employees. Many were hesitant to speak out of fear of losing their jobs. However, several spoke off the record in favor of Coke disinvestment in South Africa. A problem was the PR campaign Coke undertook among its employees to demonstrate a positive image of the role it was playing in South Africa.

Carl Ware indicated that Coke was consulting with black leadership who had encouraged Coke to remain and carry out its programs and had expressed concern that, were it to leave, it would be worse for the employees. Those he named were a bombshell to us as they included Winnie Mandela, Bishop Tutu, Alan Boesak, Persy Qhoboza, and Nthato Motlana. Carl Ware also included the name of Gatcha Buthelezi, who did not belong with this group of leaders. We did have doubts that these individuals would be speaking as Carl Ware reported.

The obtainable information and our scrutiny led us to conclude that Coke's plan fell far short of total disinvestment. It held elements of a ruse, a sham.

Coca-Cola's Divestment Plan	Our Assessment
Sell its 30% shares in major bottling company. Sell its 55% shares in canning company.	S.A. regime places severe limitations on black business development. "Divestment is not to change the color of people who finance apartheid, but to end apartheid by cutting off all corporate taxes to SA government."
Close syrup concentrate plant in Durban.	Yes, they closed the syrup plant in Durban.
Build and operate syrup plant in Swaziland with six to nine months to work out details.	Syrup supplies to South Africa bottling companies would continue.
Other Factors	**Other Factors**
Disinvest.	Distribution system remained Coke supervised. No. Coke logo remains in S.A. Coca-Cola licensing, franchising, and trademark rights remain. Coke products continued to be sold in South Africa through 15 independent bottling companies. Coke continues to market and profit.
Taxes - None paid to S. A. government.	Taxes paid to Swaziland.
	A diversionary initiative.

Investor Responsibility Research Center, Inc. (IRRC), Washington, D.C

Fact-Finding Team

One further and critical step was added. AFSC proposed and the Coalition agreed to offer to Coca-Cola a meeting with an independent, "blue ribbon" committee—a small multi-racial, gender-balanced, fact-finding team of individuals with a credible national reputation drawn from religious, church, labor, business, and public service sectors. Coke accepted the proposal. We reached out to a number of key persons to serve on the team and secured four distinguished individuals—Judge William Booth, attorney and former judge of the State of New York Criminal and Supreme Courts; Jan Douglas, consultant in national and international affairs and former Director of Community Relations for the City of Atlanta; M. William Howard, Jr., Executive Director of the Office of the Black Council, Reformed Church of America, and former President of the National Council of Churches; and Britt Pendergrast, Atlanta retired businessman and member of the Religious Society of Friends. It was December 15th, 1986 when Carl Ware, Senior Vice-President, and Brant Davis, an attorney and advisor to Coke management, met with members of the Fact-Finding Team. Stephanie Rosenthal was present to take notes.

The Fact-Finding Team issued its conclusion on December 16, 1986, with the final report published in 1987. The team's assessment coincided with that of both the Coalition and AFSC. Coke's divestment did not meet the criteria of total economic disengagement.

> The fact-finding team acknowledged that the representatives of the Coca-Cola Company seemed confident that the company had acted correctly in the best way possible, based on the establishment of the Education and Equal Opportunity Development Funds and on the decision to end all direct sales and processing of Coca-Cola in South Africa. Team members noted, however, with regard to both of these actions a number of reservations on both the nature and the progress of them. ...However, all agreed that the plan as conceived in no way approximated the usual understanding of economic withdrawal, that the company would cease to profit from the marketing of its products. Instead, it would retain exclusive relationships with marketing franchises in South Africa and its syrup concentrate for South Africa would be relocated in Swaziland, which has an economic alliance with South Africa.
>
> **Coke *Campaign*: Fact-finders Rept. 12/16/86**

Boycott Commences

Convinced that Coca-Cola believed that what they set in motion was appropriate and sufficient, on April 24, 1987 we called for the National *Boycott* of Coca-Cola products. The Coke Campaign Steering Committee believed "that it is now time to escalate the pace of the campaign to a full-fledged boycott. The Steering Committee feels that the educational work needed on disinvestment and total economic disengagement can continue while the boycott is in effect." The next day we were in Washington, DC, with banner and float, to publicize the *boycott* during a rainy and chilly day for the Mobilization for Peace and Justice in Central America and South Africa.

Coke Sweetens Apartheid

Permission of AFSC Archives

Permission of AFSC Archives

Permission of AFSC Archives

> **The Coke *Campaign*'s *Boycott* Announcement, April 24, 1987**
>
> **Following is a Statement from the Coke *Campaign*, issued today:**
>
> The Divestment Movement throughout the United States is a nonviolent strategy to bring about the desired fundamental change in South Africa. Success in the Disinvestment movement is one of the most effective building blocks toward bringing pressure on the South African government. The Coke *Campaign* is one facet of the disinvestment movement.

Reactions of Atlanta Groups to the Coke *Boycott*

SCLC was not alone among civil rights organizations to voice reluctance to join us on the *Boycott*. There was also reluctance on the part of the Martin Luther King, Jr. Center, Concerned Black Clergy, and the NAACP.

This does not discredit their significant work in the struggle against apartheid. I think they just had difficulties understanding that Coca-Cola, with such an impeccable record of supporting good causes here in the southeast region and the US in general, could in any way be associated with apartheid in South Africa. Too, Coca-Cola donated considerably, and the risk of lost funding and friendship may have been an influence.

Understanding this, we approached key leaders and requested that they remain neutral. Even if they didn't join with us, we asked that they not be openly and publicly on the side of Coca-Cola. Some people felt we were asking for something unattainable.

Reactions of South African Leaders and the ANC

As deeply disappointing as was Dr. Lowery's position were the positions taken by some prominent leaders of the anti-apartheid movement back home. It most concerned us that South African leaders, well-respected in the United States and much revered as the moral voice in South Africa, at the time when there was a vacuum caused by the ban on all political organizations, lent their support to The Coca-Cola Company.

Gloria and I were guests at a luncheon for Allan Boesak at the Atlanta Life Building on November 12, 1986 sponsored by M&M Products, Atlanta Life and The Coca-Cola Company and hosted by Mayor Andy Young. Atlanta black leadership, and political, religious, educational, and business representatives, were present. The Reverend Boesak clearly stated his approval of Coca Cola's divestment and was promoting it as a model for other multinationals. Curiously, he at the same time was critical of the General Motors withdrawal, comparing Coca-Cola as selling its stock to South African blacks whereas GM would sell to a group of whites who "in all likelihood will abandon adherence to the Sullivan Principles."

I was able to secure a ten-minute-only personal meeting with Allan in Washington to update him on the US anti-apartheid work and the *Campaign*'s direction. He seemed unflinching in his support of Coca-Cola.

It was further on that Archbishop Tutu wrote a strong letter of support for Coke and criticism of those who impugned his integrity for involvement in the Equal Opportunity Fund (April 10, 1989). Coca-Cola circulated that letter throughout the United States saying, "The AFSC and Coca-Cola *boycott* group, don't know what they're talking about. The legitimate voice for South Africans is in the struggle there and stating what needs to be done and that voice is Bishop Tutu."

This was difficult. Coke's promotion of Reverend Tutu's letter was a huge distraction and worked to our disadvantage. Winning Bishop Tutu and others to its side increased the tendency for *Boycott* supporters to start aiming criticism toward Tutu. We reversed this course: our response was to expend energy on Coke's position and seek higher moral ground by calling attention to Tutu's support of the sanctions movement rather than to his failure to support the *Boycott*.

I believe Coca-Cola, intentionally or unintentionally, did quite a bit to cause divisions within the anti-apartheid movement in an attempt to defuse attention on themselves by creating a red herring. We believed that Coca-Cola was trying not only to divide opinion but incredibly to mislead.

We were particularly disappointed not to find public support from the African National Congress. For years we had encouraged their interest and support, ideally with written confirmation. This did not occur. In 1983, we had decided to make a direct approach to the ANC in their New York City office. As the date approached, I made a strategic decision to remain behind and asked Gloria to go in my stead with Moriba Karamoko, AFSC's Assistant Regional Director in Atlanta, to talk with Thabo Mbeki. They made the case for ANC support of the *Campaign* but received no commitments.

Later, and only verbally, did representatives explain to us that, as the main liberation movement, it was not easy to endorse each boycott or other activity around the world. They said that we did have their endorsement as long as we were undertaking the *Boycott* under the umbrella of sanctions.

Coke Free Zones and *Boycott*

With the announcement, we moved full swing into the boycott phase. Already boycott actions were occurring spontaneously in other parts of the country. Makini Coleman was succeeded by Malkia M'Buzi Moore as the Coordinator, and Malkia was later followed by Soter Irusota. All these devoted individuals faced the rigors of demanding responsibilities and modest or non-existent economic resources to pay their salaries.

High school and college students, religious orders, and unions were major players. The *Campaign* provided an effective tool to learn about and speak against apartheid, to pressure for sanctions and disinvestment. To boycott Coke products and create *Coke Free Zones* often required rigorous protocols of the democratic process—discussions, debates, referendums, and votes. Individuals wrote letters to the *Campaign* describing their individual boycott of Coke, often with copies to Carl Ware.

Partial List of Sites of Coke *Boycott* Actions

1985
Georgia State University, Student Government Association

1986
Clark College — Atlanta, GA
Columbia University — New York, NY
Compton College — California — *Coke Free Zone*
Georgia State University — Students Coalition Against Apartheid and Racism (SCAAR)
Howard University — Washington, DC
Mary Washington — Virginia
Michigan State
Morehouse College — Atlanta, GA — call for removal of Coke machines

South Africa *Boycott* Committee (SABOC) — New York, NY — (American and African Students met at International House), boycotted Coke
Tennessee State

1987
Johns Hopkins University — Maryland — students request removal — CC reps visit
Plaquemine Parish, Louisiana's Students' Action on Coke Boycott Portland HS, OR

1988
Johns Hopkins University, Baltimore, MD — publicity
LeMoyne College — Syracuse, NY — publicity
Notre Dame — Indiana — publicity
Towson State University's *Townson's University Press* — Maryland — publicity
University of Massachusetts, African Students Organization — publicity

1989
Amherst College — Massachusetts
Boeing Aircraft's Black Employees endorsed *Boycott*
Cambridge Rindge and Latin High School — Massachusetts — vote to boycott Coca-Cola products and machines at school
Cleveland High School, Roosevelt High School, Lincoln working toward Coke-free Zone
Hampshire College — Massachusetts
Michigan State University
Davis Food Co-op — Davis, California
Mount Holyoke College — Massachusetts
Penn State — Pennsylvania — Committee for Justice in South Africa
Smith College — Massachusetts
Spelman College — Atlanta, GA
Spelman College — Community Conference "Working to End Apartheid"
University of Massachusetts, Amherst, MA
University of Texas — Texas Union Board of Directors decision not to renew Coke contract

Map by Laura McIntyre

1990

Archdiocese and food service employees – Chicago, IL – remove Coca Cola machines

Black employees of Boeing Aircraft – Seattle, WA – endorse *Campaign* and *boycott* products

George Washington High School – Denver, CO – Coke machines removed from student lounges

Georgetown Day School – Washington, DC – Coke machines removed

Haverford College, Haverford, PA – students worked to convince two student operations to stop selling Coke

High School for Hispanic – Chicago, IL – remove Coca-Cola machines

Hyatt Regency Hotel – Oakland, CA – remove Coca-Cola machine during Mandela's stay

Portland State – Washington protests – PS Coke *Boycott* Coalition

Saint Scholastic – Chicago, IL – *Boycott* – show "Last Grave at Dimbaza" to incoming students

Springfield College – voted to ban Coca-Cola on campus

University of Connecticut – question Coca-Cola on campus as school fully divested

1991

Springfield School Committee (Public Schools), Springfield, MA – exploring *Boycott*

St. Louis Community College Forest Park, IL

Speaking Engagements

I traveled throughout the country to meet with as many audiences as possible, as did *Campaign* staff and volunteers. Wherever I addressed an audience on apartheid, I made sure to highlight the Coca-Cola *Campaign*. Soon AFSC's staff in other regional offices added the *Campaign* and *Boycott* support to their program responsibilities, creating hubs of activity in Cambridge, Baltimore, and Portland as well as Philadelphia.

We paid attention to the invitations Coca-Cola accepted to speak to students on their role in South Africa: December 1, 1987 – Johns Hopkins, January 12, 1989 – Cambridge Rindge and Latin School, and January 3, 1991 – Springfield School Committee. These public presentations by Coke confirmed to us that they were paying attention to the *Boycott*, that it mattered to them.

On occasions both Carl Ware and I were invited to present our distinct views together before student bodies. Local press seemed eager to cover. Throughout these engagements there was no acrimony, no personal ill-feeling. I'm not sure there was any instance when his views prevailed in the final student vote to boycott.

Cambridge Rindge and Latin School Highlight

I share an example of student engagement in the *Boycott*, which speaks to the work by the students and their school community, by Coca-Cola and by the *Campaign* itself.

In the fall of 1988, students of the Cambridge Rindge and Latin School began the study of apartheid and a discussion of participation in the Coca-Cola *Boycott*. When *Boycott* posters began to appear, a Coke supplier complained they were pasted on Coke soda machines. Talks led to a decision to host a debate. I accepted the invitation to present along with Carl Ware and Joseph Thloloe, a school parent and prominent journalist who had spent years in South African jails for his political views.

The vote took place on February 13, 1989 with a 3-1 margin in favor of the *Boycott* of products and removal of machines from the campus.

Coca-Cola Efforts to Dissuade and Intimidate Coke *Boycott* Supporters

Coca-Cola used intimidating tactics with our boycott committee. In fact, the Coalition's Gloria Gaines, who also served as the chairperson of the Coca-Cola *Boycott* Committee, heard from her boss at MARTA of a call from Carl Ware making MARTA aware of Gloria's involvement in the anti-apartheid movement and the Coke *Campaign*. That was intended, perhaps, to be a threat. Thankfully, her boss, Morris J. Dillard, Deputy General Manager, was understanding of it all. As a former SNCC activist, he understood, as Gloria said, "that there was my professional side as well as my activist side and he just said to me to be careful."

Gloria was not the only one; there were a few others who reported similar attempts to intimidate. Professor Mack Jones of Atlanta University was another such person. We learned that Carl Ware had called the president of Clark Atlanta

University suggesting that he discipline his professors. According to Mack, the president was not bothered by the call, and he did not tell us to "back-off," which is likely what Ware would like to have seen happen.

Coca-Cola had mistaken the character of our Atlanta leaders. These individuals did not cease their support for the struggle, and I admire that. Nor did they lose their jobs. In some ways, for an activist to be targeted by Coke could be considered a badge of honor. Our folks were obviously intimidating the mammoth Coca-Cola Company.

Later Years of the *Boycott*

The release of Nelson Mandela in February 1990 understandably raised the question, "What now?" For many in the anti-apartheid movement, his release brought change if not an ending to their most active work.

Yet, the dismantling of the apartheid regime required vigilance and constant pressure. We agreed to continue our pressures through the *Campaign*. In his address to the United Nations Security Council on July 15, 1990, Nelson Mandela remarked, "We should like sanctions to be reimposed," a reflection in response to the George H.W. Bush administration's decision to lift sanctions.

Coke *Campaign* constituents received my periodic general statements and news releases on the status of negotiations, the beginning dismantlement of apartheid laws, the hard road ahead for South Africa. All the while we encouraged public continuation of the *Boycott*.

> **AFSC Atlanta News Release, June 13, 1990**
> Nelson Mandela's release from prison and the lifting of the state of emergency are most hopeful signs that the abolition of apartheid and freedom for 25 million black South Africans is within reach. But we are not ready to fully celebrate. Major obstacles remain. Nelson Mandela cannot yet vote. Other political prisoners are still in jail.
>
> Until such time as Mr. Mandela and his country people fully participate in the decision making of their country, and while he, the ANC, and the UN support continued sanctions, Coca-Cola remains in a difficult position.
>
> We urge The Coca-Cola Company, during these critical times, to make a dramatic gesture of support for apartheid's demise by withdrawing fully from South Africa. Withdrawal of Coke products from the stadiums in which Mr. Mandela will speak in the U.S. would be a dramatic and firm statement of the Company's resolve and support for the abolition of apartheid.

Letter to Supporters, March 11, 1991
As of yet, the SA Government has to agree to the ANC conditions to negotiations for an Interim Government and an elected constituent assembly to manage the transition from minority to majority rule.... Black South Africans have asked that we maintain present sanctions, divestiture and boycotts, until they attain their full democratic rights....

May 19, 1993
Dear Colleague,

I want to respond to your inquiry on the status of the coke *boycott campaign*. The *campaign* was initiated in the 1985 based on the premise that sanctions, divestment, and international boycotts are an effective non-violent strategy to isolate the apartheid regime and thereby promote fundamental change in South Africa.

While the *boycott* committee recognizes that a measure of progress toward democracy in South Africa has been achieved through the repeal of the most virulent apartheid laws, we acknowledge that de facto apartheid remains entrenched, and virtually unscathed.

Therefore, the *boycott* of all Coca-Cola products will proceed until an interim government and democratically-elected constituent assembly are established. We encourage U.S. citizens to stand in solidarity with the South African liberation leaders who have upheld sanctions. In an address to the United Nations Security Council, African National Congress president Nelson Mandela criticized the Bush administration's South Africa policy and remarked, "We would like sanctions to be reimposed."

We await eagerly the day when economic pressure is no longer necessary, and a democratic, non-racial South Africa replaces the current and continuing reality of apartheid.

Thank you for your past efforts and your present interest. If you have any further questions or concerns, please do not hesitate to contact us.

Aluta continua,
Thandi Gcabashe / Coordinator Coke *Boycott Campaign*

Nelson Mandela, the ANC, and Coca-Cola Divestment

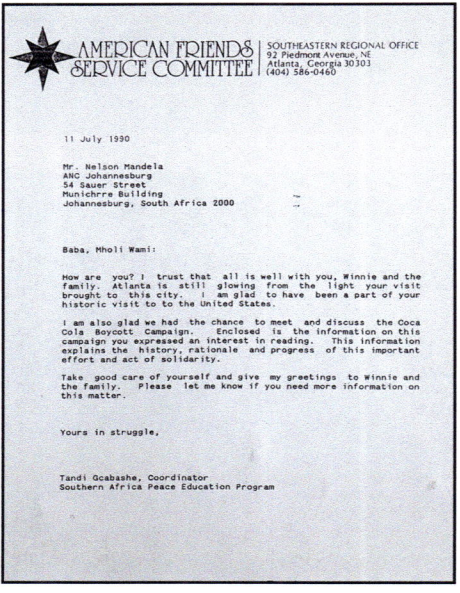

I have to say that Nelson Mandela himself was principled on the issue of this *Boycott*. He arrived for the 1990 independence celebrations in Namibia in a Coca-Cola jet. He was told of the *Boycott*, and he did not return home to South Africa in a Coca-Cola jet.

During Mandela's 1990 visit to the US, Coca-Cola extended offers of assistance, which he and the ANC turned down. In Atlanta, as elsewhere on his eight-city tour, the community poured out to streets and venues to welcome him. Nelson requested of the Atlanta host committee not to allow the sale of Coca-Cola at his speaking venues. It took some pressure on the Georgia Tech administrators, but the host committee succeeded in having Coca-Cola billboards covered when Mandela spoke to an audience of 50,000 at the Georgia Tech Bobby Dodd Stadium. At appearances in New York, California, and Atlanta, boycott supporters carried multi-colored balloons with a picture of Nelson on one side and the words "*Boycott* Coca-Cola" on the other. The *Atlanta Journal and Constitution* on June 13, wrote:

> The African National Congress has rejected efforts by the Coca-Cola Co. to buy into Nelson Mandela's U.S. tour. …Organizers rebuffed Coke's offers to provide a corporate plane for the ANC leader and to raise money for the ANC. A Coke official insisted, however, that talks were continuing…Mr. Mandela will tour from June 20 to July 1 to press for continued sanctions against companies doing business in South Africa.

Such incidents may appear to be small victories, but when facing Goliath small victories amount to a lot. I thought this was a real encouragement for the *Boycott*.

I don't wish to speculate on what other reasons there might have been for the ANC's lack of formal support for the Coke *Boycott*. Later on, we were again disappointed when the *Boycott* was continuing and sanctions were still pursued. Negotiations had begun in South Africa, and the chief representative of the ANC in Washington, DC wrote a letter endorsing The Coca-Cola Company. It wasn't clear that the letter was against the *Boycott*. It was written very carefully, but it was clear in support of Coca-Cola. That was disturbing. But, as I say, it was late in the game and the whole sanctions pressure was, at that point, fading.

End of the *Campaign*

In the later years the Georgia Coalition saw its membership diminish in numbers. So many individuals had given so much of their time and energies over the years, working side by side with me in so many ways, and many remained individually engaged.

AFSC, my employer, had been a major player in partnership with Georgia Coalition members. As a national organization with policies on disinvestment and internal processes for Board decisions, it deliberatively consulted widely before officially deciding to co-sponsor the *Campaign* in 1986 and then the *Boycott* in July 1987, several months after the Coalition's call. Among other contributions were Jerry Herman's leadership as national staff for Southern Africa Program in the Philadelphia headquarters, AFSC staff throughout the US, and AFSC's fiscal and administrative sensibilities.

By July 1993, the AFSC, and many other such national and international organizations, were preparing to receive official word from South African religious and anti-apartheid leaders asking that sanctions be lifted, and companies reinvest in the newly democratic nation. We concluded to bring the *Campaign* to a close:

> ... and dedicate ourselves to the remaining task of continuing sanctions until the majority are confident that the changes in South Africa are irreversible, and the next task: supporting free and fair elections and preparing to assist a new majority-led government in South Africa as it seeks to build a just society.

By the fall of 1993, in his long-awaited and now famous speech of September 24th to the UN Apartheid Committee, in the vast meeting hall of the UN General Assembly to accommodate all those interested, Nelson Mandela called for an end to sanctions.

> In response to the historic advances toward democracy that have been achieved and to help create the necessary conditions for stability and social progress, we believe the time has come when the international community should lift all economic sanctions against South Africa.

1996 Evaluation of Coca-Cola *Boycott Campaign*

Three years later, in 1996 before my return home, we convened on September 21, some of the major players to evaluate the *Campaign*'s many elements and identify the lessons learned for any future campaign work. In my invitation I stressed the meeting's intent:

> To be a serious sharing of our experiences and recollections of the *campaign*, and an examination of how that experience could be of use to AFSC in the future. Equally important, it should be a reunion and celebration of us, the key players, who made the *campaign* a worthwhile undertaking.

Seated in AFSC Atlanta Office Conference Room, beginning top left, Carol Luther, Kuhusu Wanzu, Malkia M'Buzi Moore, Ken Martin, Bill Holland, Frances Crowe, Jerry Herman, Thandi. Not shown, Gloria Gaines and Elizabeth Enloe

Permission of Elizabeth Enloe

Committed to as much candor as possible, around the tables in the AFSC Atlanta office were myself, Malkia, Gloria, Elizabeth, Kuhusu Wanzu, Bill Holland, Frances Crowe, Jerry Herman, Ken Martin, and Carol Luther.

A written record has not surfaced so I reflect, with the benefit of notes, that Jerry Herman beautifully focused us on the people involved from the beginnings of the anti-apartheid movement in South Africa up and through the *Campaign*. We pieced together the chronology and examined major elements such as: strategic focus on education and partnerships, clarity of purpose, conscientious examination of facts, attention to world forces and local needs, engagement with the ANC and other liberation movements, AFSC's organizational structures, headquarter office in the heart of Atlanta, financial strains, commitment of volunteers, and the elusive use of the term "we" in the mutually beneficial relationship between the Georgia Coalition for Divestment in South Africa and the AFSC.

When we undertook the *Coca-Cola Campaign and Boycott* there were many people saying, "You can't do it. It's too much." Some thought we were crazy. Yet, it was a David and Goliath analogy. The *Boycott* had pay-offs. A lot of people ultimately admired the effort. Students were excited. Individuals had something to put their hands on and be involved. All it took was to not put fifty cents into the slots of Coca-Cola machines. If your conscience says you should act, if your analysis says you should do it, plunge in, and give it your all.

The nine years of the *Campaign* between 1984 and 1993 were intense.
We did not succeed in securing Coca-Cola's complete divestment from South Africa.
However, if we were to make only one claim of victory
as to the *Campaign*'s success,
it would be its ability to make visible the horror of apartheid,
and to make possible for thousands of people in the United States
their meaningful opposition to the atrocities in South Africa.

Part IV

After Nelson's Release, 1990 - 1996

13

Nelson's Release and Beyond, Last Years of Apartheid

"Nelson Is Free But He Cannot Vote"

The most important and exhilarating development arrived with the release of Nelson Mandela, on February 11th, 1990. An elated and fascinated world welcomed him to freedom.

When I began work full time in 1981, Nelson was on Robben Island with ANC leaders Walter Sisulu, Govan Mbeki, and others serving a life sentence. P. W. Botha of the National Party was serving as the Prime Minister of the apartheid government. Ronald Reagan was the newly elected President of the United States who promoted the policy of constructive engagement.

My thoughts contradicted themselves as to when the end of apartheid would occur. When first in exile, I thought apartheid would topple in five or ten years and I would return home. But the apartheid regime was belligerent. I found myself in the United States for twenty-six years and there were times that I could not say with assurance that I expected South

Permission of AFSC Archives

Africa to change in my lifetime. Simply, I did the work that needed to be done from day to day to put pressure on apartheid.

When the actual change came about, the final downfall of apartheid, it happened so quickly it was almost unbelievable. The watershed moment was the day Nelson walked out of prison. That's when we knew that things would never be the same, that we had entered an irreversible course. Yet it happened so fast. We didn't believe Nelson was really released. Then we entered formal negotiations that lasted four years, and then came the elections in 1994. We still really didn't believe that change was happening. But once it started it just snowballed, and it was beautiful, and we were incredulous—the downfall was happening.

The flood of media interest demanded my attention. Old constituencies felt a need for analysis and discussion of the developments. Newly interested individuals were emotionally moved by the selfless life story of Mandela. Immediately, I was thrust into so many speaking engagements that we discussed a public relations firm or agent to assist. Between February 11 and the remainder of the month of February I addressed 25 audiences.

Notwithstanding the elation, we were clear that not-so-easy steps had to be undertaken before apartheid was fully dismantled. The rush of nations and corporations to revoke sanctions was almost immediate despite ANC's request that it was too soon.

The oppressive and repressive conditions that Nelson bravely opposed—and that he went to jail for—still prevailed. He had been released from his jail cell into the larger prison of South Africa.

In the early 1990s, I kept abreast of unfolding events, closely monitoring on-going negotiations and later the transition planning. My emphasis changed to meet the interests of concerned Americans and share the nature and status of the negotiations and transition process from apartheid white rule to a multiparty democracy.

For the next six years I traveled widely. I responded to speaking engagement requests, explained the importance of continued sanctions and the Coke Campaign, organized the commemorative events, hosted distinguished guests, and promoted the on-going Sister City Braklaagte Project. I traveled home five times – to attend the South African Council of Churches, the African National Congress, and the Congress of South African Unions conferences in 1990; to take part with ANC members during the first Annual Conference of the ANC inside the country since its banning in 1960; to accompany an AFSC fact-finding delegation to study South African violence in 1992; to participate in a 200-member observer team for the 1994 elections and to vote; and, finally, to observe local municipal elections in 1995.

Namibia's Independence, Meeting Mandela and Conferring with Anti-Apartheid Leadership in South Africa 1990

I accepted the honor of President Sam Nujoma's invitation to attend the four-day festivities in March 1990 in Windhoek the capital, on the occasion of Namibia's

Nelson's Release and Beyond, Last Years of Apartheid 141

independence celebrations. It was there that I greeted Nelson in person, one month after his release from prison.

Immediately after the celebrations and in South Africa, I consulted with Nelson and with other leaders regarding the violence and ravaged areas of Natal. The message I heard directly from the membership of the Mass Democratic Movement, the Congress of South African Trade Unions, and the South African Council of Churches was: "Thandi, the 1986 U.S. sanctions legislation, weak as it was and reluctantly enforced by the Reagan administration, has brought the regime to the negotiating table." Aware that the authorities did not come to the peace table willingly, the regime should not be allowed to regress by easing sanctions. Rather than relax sanctions, we needed to intensify them.

Nelson and Winne Mandela World Speaking Tour— Atlanta Visit – 1990

Before my trip to Namibia and in anticipation of Nelson's 1990 worldwide speaking tour, the Nelson Mandela Reception Committee was formed worldwide—in Amsterdam, London, Stockholm, Oslo, New York, Los Angeles, Tokyo, and Austin.

In Atlanta, I was asked to convene a similar reception committee and we undertook several initial steps to immediately celebrate Nelson's release and to educate people about the struggle for freedom. Throughout the intervening months,

Atlanta Airport on June 27, 1990. Arrival of Nelson Mandela and Winnie Mandela. Governor Joe Frank Harris, Fulton County Commission Chairman Michael Lomax, Valerie R. Jackson, Winnie Mandela, Nelson Mandela, Mayor Maynard Jackson, Coretta Scott King, secret service agent, Harry and Julie Belafonte

Permission of Susan J. Ross

I was deeply involved in advising and planning the demanding set of scheduled events for Nelson and Winnie Mandela's June 1990 visit. The AFSC office served as a focal point for information, requests, and opinion venting.

At the invitation of Mayor Maynard Jackson, I was present at Hartsfield Atlanta International Airport on June 27th when the Mandelas arrived, and I was pleased to attend a number of the day's many events. It was a demanding day for the Mandelas, and a day of exhilaration for those thousands of people who came greet them.

Our unique engagement focused on the intricacies and sensitivities around Coca-Cola which I've described in an earlier chapter. As chairperson of the host committee, Mrs. King stated her disappointment with the *Atlanta Journal Constitution's* characterization of the ANC's rebuff of Coca-Cola's offers of assistance. She wrote:

> I know of no other company among the 587 U.S. companies with business in South Africa that have done as much to support the struggle against apartheid and lay the foundations for a post-apartheid South Africa…. I feel that the *Constitution* owes its readers a more thoughtful consideration of Coca-Cola's impressive leadership in the area of corporate responsibility.

Mrs. King and Nelson Mandela

Winnie Mandela with Thandi

Thandi with the Reverend Joseph Lowery

David Ndaba/Sam Gulube

All photos Permission by Susan J. Ross

Atlanta South African Community

Sanctions Campaign and the Coca-Cola Boycott Continue

Nelson Mandela spoke directly about sanctions in his speech to the world through the United Nations Security Council on July 15, 1990, after 27 years of imprisonment.

> We call on the international community to continue the campaign to isolate the regime. To lift sanctions now would be to run the risk of aborting the process toward the complete eradication of apartheid.

Pressures to ensure complete dismantling of apartheid were needed. We determined to concentrate on analysis and education and to intensify our efforts to uphold the sanctions campaign and the Coca-Cola Boycott, through updates, speaking engagements, and support to schools still in negotiation for Coke Free Zones.

ANC Conference in South Africa and Report - July 1991

When I returned home again in July 1991, the circumstances were historic and radically different. Mandela was present, and exiled South Africans were coming home. The conference was abuzz with excitement for those who had lived in exile. It was the first time that we as exiles met freely with those United Democratic Front members and others who had fought from within.

One of the hot issues on the agenda was the level of representation of women in the top structures of the ANC. The Women's League was pushing for 30% representation in all of those positions, and there was strong resistance from our male compatriots such that the debate went into the wee hours of the night. The discussion was lengthy and extremely challenging until some in the Youth League intervened and the opposition finally conceded to the women's demand. And, by the way, the demand increased from 30% to 50%. Perhaps one day gender equality will cease to be a contentious issue.

The 2,244 delegates eventually affirmed these resolutions:

- Maintain international sanctions
- Government must end political violence
- Elect constituent assembly
- Write new constitution
- Form transitional government

It felt so good to move about freely in my native country without any restrictions or informers and spies trailing after me. It was extremely liberating. This was the first time I was actually a free citizen of my own country.

One memory that stands out is my visit to the beachfront in Durban, where I observed throngs of black people swimming. They of their own volition had decided to disregard the "Europeans Only" signs and desegregated the beaches. What stunned me most was not just the act of desegregation, but a realization of how unrealistic, stupid, and ill-conceived the policy of apartheid had been. Mathematically, it had been a pipe dream to wish away South African citizens, who comprised 80% of the population.

Here below is an excerpt of my report on my 1991 visit, which I presented to the AFSC's Board members and staff in Philadelphia, and the AFSC Atlanta Executive Committee:

> I could not believe that towards the end of my three months visit in South Africa I began to feel home sick. South Africans would respond to my nostalgia by asking - "What do you mean that you are home sick?" I had to explain that I have a job to keep, and that although one daughter has repatriated, I still have three children who reside in the USA. Furthermore, after 20 years of exile, living in Atlanta, I have acquired many friends of whom I am deeply fond. I am truly glad to be back amongst all of you.
>
> You have supported our struggle for freedom, liberations, and equality, for so long and so faithfully that I need to tell you this because people at home greatly appreciate the campaigns you have waged on our behalf, particularly in the area of sanctions.
>
> I took this trip as you know under the auspices of the AFSC and would like to thank the SERO Executive Committee for concurring with the decision to grant me this opportunity. AFSC felt that due to the de Klerk announcements regarding change and reform in SA, a fact-finding mission should be undertaken. We needed to know what changes had occurred, what they meant and what their implications and ramifications are for the oppressed people of South Africa.
>
> In 1989 because mother was seriously ill, the South African authorities granted me a visa for a 30-day visit. This brief trip was taken under very careful and guarded circumstances, as I was still considered an exile.
>
> I could return now because the de Klerk government announced on the 2nd of February 1990 the unbanning of political organizations and individuals; the lifting of the state of emergency; the releasing of political prisoners and the scrapping of the Separate Public Amenities Act. Exiles who met the indemnity requirements could also return.
>
> In 1991 de Klerk was widely applauded for repealing what was notoriously referred to as "Pillars of Apartheid." These were composed of The Group Areas Act, which allowed for residential separation according to race; The Land Acts of 1913 & 1936 which divided the land mass into 87% for 16% white people and 13% for 84% black people; The Population Registration which required classification according to race at birth; the Reservation of Separate Amenities Act that enforced petty apartheid; The Natives Land Act which made it illegal for Africans to own land in urban areas.

To be fair, objective, and impartial to the Government of South Africa, we need to recognize and acknowledge that some changes did occur. But equally important in order to be fair to the people of South Africa, we need to analyze these changes, in an attempt to separate myth from fact and reality. My presentation will attempt to draw your attention to the subtleness of the present conditions in SA.

I attended three conferences of the South African Council of Churches, the African National Congress, and the Congress of South African unions. A more expansive report will be available at a later date.

In order to gain a fairly representative opinion on current conditions, status of changes and prospects for the future, I spoke and listened carefully to many individuals and groups from a broad spectrum, black and white.

The black community is frustrated, angry and experiencing enormous disillusion with the whole process of change. The euphoria and excitement the people felt when Nelson was released is diminishing and quickly slipping away. Regarding de Klerk's promise of a New South Africa, they feel it is nowhere near or imminent for them. A common phrase is 'DASHED HOPES.'

In the white community, there are four identifiable political camps. The majority are Afrikaner "moderate" who support de Klerk's views within the Nationalist Party's political framework. The next sizable group consists of members of the "Liberal" party who persistently opposed sanctions during the heyday of apartheid. This group condemned some of the harsh and discomforting aspects of apartheid but remained loyal to the country and are extremely protective of the country's wealth. The third group is a small fringe group of right wingers that unabashedly flaunt white supremacy insignia and views in public. They feel de Klerk has sold out on the white nation. The fourth group are those whites who have thrown their lot unreservedly with the oppressed masses with commitment to unconditional dismantling of apartheid and replacing it with a nonracial, nonsexist, democratic south Africa.

Commemorative Events

The commemorations of Sharpeville and Soweto continued at least through 1992, bringing to Atlanta on March 21, 1991 two South African speakers, one affiliated with the Azania Peoples Organization (AZAPO), and the other a member of the ANC Working Group preparing for negotiations; and in March 1992 Imani Countess with her keynote address, "South Africa in Transition," after which a new community support group formed calling itself Atlantans for Democracy in Southern Africa. The Boipatong Massacre of June 17, 1992 brought us together once again:

> We join the people of South Africa today in mourning the 48 innocent men, women and children who died in the state-sponsored massacre at Boipatong township on June 17. They are among the more than 6,000 people who have

died in apartheid violence since Nelson Mandela's release from prison two years ago. – an act the white minority regime promised would usher in in a 'season of Peace." …We join the African National Congress, the Congress of South African Trade Unions, the South African Council of Churches, and many millions of ordinary South Africans in demanding an end to the violence and the establishment of a multi-racial interim government to guide the nation to genuine democracy. We urge our Senators to co-sponsor Senate Resolution 301, which puts responsibility for the killing where it belongs – on the white government – and calls on the Bush Administration to support the people's demands for peace and liberty. …. Above all we call on the apartheid regime to stop the training, financing and arming of death squads and vigilante gangs and bring its security forces under international supervision and control.

Chris Hani – Memorial Service, AFSC offices - April 19, 1993

A program report stated: Thandi Gcabashe, director of the Southern Africa Program of AFSC who visited with Chris Hanni on her 1991 trip to South Africa, lamented that; "He was a robust, energetic, jovial man, popular with the youth due to his ability to relate to their hopelessness and sense of frustration." Ms. Gcabashe added that his death is particularly disturbing because he alone had the ability to contain the anger and bitterness of the youth.

Permission of AFSC Archives

Distinguished Visitors

The number of distinguished persons visiting Atlanta was considerable during these years and we were instrumental in the organization and facilitation of these visits.

We hosted **Dr. Kristasamy**, a member of CHISA, Coalition for Health in South Africa. The groups worked on issues related to health in post-apartheid South Africa. The Program and the National Black Women's Health Project co-hosted 30 South African leaders who worked on grassroots community activities geared towards self-sufficiency and economic independence.

Program committee members co-hosted **ANC Deputy President Walter Sisulu's** visit to Atlanta and successfully organized a public reception at Morris Brown College. Staff arranged for and escorted the visitors to a church service by Dr. Lowery, and a luncheon at the Carter Center.

Dinner for Bishop and Mrs. Tutu in Thandi's Home
Permission of Gloria Gaines

Dr. Sibusiso Vil-Nkomo, an exile and victim of the uprisings, then associate professor at Lincoln University and Specialist in International political economy and Policy analysis, gave an excellent update of the then current peace negotiations. Workshops and cultural presentations were part of the ceremony.

Bishop Tutu's three-month sabbatical at Emory University offered the Program a rare opportunity to bring community activists and the Bishop together at a reception at my Atlanta home.

AFSC's Ozong Agborsangaya coordinated the month-long southeastern tour of **Nomalanga Mosala**, member of the ANC and Chair of the ANC Women's League who had fought to overcome the pass laws and advocated for women in unions, for fair salaries, for preschool daycare and improved quality of education.

The Program cosponsored a delegation of **28 clergy from the Dutch Reformed Church** in South Africa, jointly with the American Jewish Committee and six other religious and social change organizations based in Atlanta for dinner discussion of "Reconciliation in Post-Apartheid South Africa."

Numerous other prominent visitors were hosted by the Southern Africa Program, amongst whom was **Dr. Wilmot James, director of the Institute for a Democratic South Africa** (IDASA), who promoted processes that transform institutions and communities.

AFSC Delegation to Study Violence in South Africa (1992)

In 1992, I accompanied an AFSC six-member fact finding team of US and South African members (4 Americans, 2 South Africans from the SA Council of Churches) with the purpose of studying the violence in black townships that had become a

destabilizing factor in the negotiations. The delegation produced its report, to be widely circulated, "Politics of Hope and Fear: South Africa in Transition," in November 1992. A program report stated:

The team was directed by the AFSC Board to investigate the sources of the violence, where it originates, what was its purpose and how the continuing violence affected the transition process. The hope of the study tour was to create a fair report of the conflict. The team travelled widely in South Africa, interviewing representatives of the government (police, military, government officials, homeland leaders and homeland police), change organizations (African National Congress and allies, labor unions, South African Communist Party), and other groups (Pan Africanist Congress, Inkatha Freedom Party, youth groups, women's groups).

Tandi noted that the economy of South Africa was under great stress. Massive unemployment and rising inflation have placed a great burden on many. Several factors contribute to the bad economic prospect: the climate of violence discourages investment, mismanagement by the government and the impact of sanctions.

Politically, there is no outside signs of apartheid, but the practice of apartheid remains. Blacks are still unable to vote in South Africa.

Media attention has tended to define the violence in South Africa as " black on black violence." Tandi encouraged the committee (AFSC Executive Committee) to view the violence as between the forces of the status quo (government, homelands, police, and military) and the forces of change. Black persons serve both the status quo and the forces for change. The study committee recommendations are included in the report. There needs to be: 1) a transition of power, 2) international monitoring and 3) a strong United States policy for South Africa.

The Southern Africa Peace Education Program is planning a speaking tour in the spring to report on their findings.

King Center Sends Delegation Headed By Andrew Young - 1993

The King Center, recognizing that South Africans would be responsible for delivering local government services in a still hostile environment, sent a delegation to KwaZulu. The group was headed by Andrew Young and the Reverend James Orange, and made up of members of various sectors of local government, including Gloria Gaines representing the transportation sector.

Election Observer and Casting My Vote - 1994

My next visit home was in 1994, to observe and vote in the first democratic elections in South Africa. I share details of this experience in Chapter 15, and the full text of my report in the Appendices. For the present I include this undated 1994 letter to my AFSC colleagues:

To: Bill Holland and Executive Committee Members

On April 15th, I will be traveling to South Africa with a delegation under the auspices of the Africana Women Studies, Clark Atlanta University to monitor the South African Elections.

This delegation and others of its kind help ensure that the elections on April 27, 1994 will be free and fair. This trip has special significance for all those who have worked for years to see the end of apartheid in South Africa. But for South Africans like myself, who were privy to and lived through that social system of injustice, war, and racism, this is a profound moment.

To return to South Africa to cast a vote denotes that end of the apartheid era and my life's ambition to purge South Africa of a system that saw to my exile, the end of my father's life, and those of the many South Africans who were committed to rid South Africa of its diabolical treatment of its black citizens. This is an impassioned victory.

Well… I recognize the struggle is not done. But the apartheid regime is over. My forefathers and all the soldiers of the anti-apartheid movement who died can rest in peace. Now the struggle for me and other South African(s) will be to create conditions for equity and peace that will work for all South Africans. We much pass the lessons that we have learned to our children and all the children of South Africa. They can carry on the work for peace not only for themselves but for all the people of the world.

Upon my return to Atlanta program work moved at a normal pace. In the last three months of the year, we lectured in 3 high schools; at the University of North Carolina and Johnson C. Smith College in Charlotte; Georgia State University; and at Chapman and California Tech in California. The topics were varied and interesting, ranging from: "Analysis of South Africa's Elections", to "Challenges Facing the New South Africa", to Prospects for Prosperity in South Africa: social/political/economic."

Looking Forward, 1995 - 1996
Observation of South African Local Elections - 1995

There was one more visit home before returning permanently. I enjoyed a sabbatical of several months in 1995, some of which was spent observing the highly charged

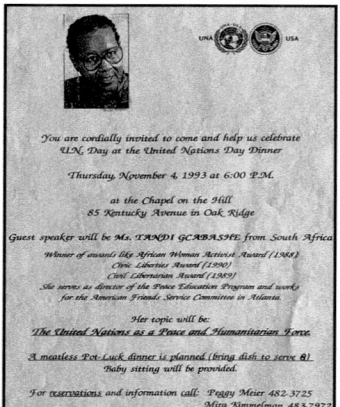 

AFSC Southern Africa Task Force Meeting, New York City, October 1983. Thandi with Frances Crowe in middle. Jerry Herman back row right

Photo by David Gracie. Permission of AFSC Archives

November 1st local elections where citizens, including myself, voted in newly integrated municipalities. The significance of the placement of elected mayors and councils was the capacity to deliver upon the ANC's Reconstruction and Development Program.

It was not until 1996 that I returned home. Until then I used my time to influence the shape of AFSC's continued support to South Africa with its vast new challenges. I submitted a program proposal focused on continued education and on engagement with South African communities such as Braklaagte. The proposal won approval, and thus committed funds, to continue on-going attention to South Africa from the Atlanta office.

14

Visits Home to South Africa and International Travel

1972 – The first time I went home to South Africa after going into exile was in 1972. My mother-in-law was sick, and she made a passionate plea to see our two older girls. I enlisted the assistance of an influential white South African who resided in Atlanta to secure a one-way emergency travel document into South Africa. As I recall the entire circumstance, I was homesick at that time. I traveled with the two children, and encountered problems on my return to Atlanta. I lingered and lingered in South Africa while the South African government refused to supply me with a one-way return document. It was clear that the authorities were determined to deny me consideration. But, in due course, with influential persons in South Africa intervening, a liberal member of the South African parliament succeeded in making the government yield.

1985 – I attended the United Nations Decade for Women World Conference in Nairobi, Kenya. A delegation from Atlanta also attended, including Gloria Gaines and Makini Coleman.

1987 – I traveled to Europe for vacation and extended the time to publicize the Coke Campaign Boycott. I held meetings with anti-apartheid organizations in London, West Germany, and in Geneva where I met with Jean Sindab, Director of the Progamme to Combat Racism of the World Council of Churches, with whom I worked when she was director of the Washington Office on Africa.

1989 – The next visit home was in 1989 when my Mom was very sick after a mild heart attack and was in the hospital. She sent a message that she wanted to see me so I did all I could to be with her. It was still difficult to secure a visa to enter South Africa since I was a "prohibited" person (a black South African affiliated with the African National Congress and engaged in organizing against apartheid while in the United States). In dealing with the on-going resistance and refusal from the South

Thandi with her mother, Nokukhanya Luthuli

Permission of Gcabashe Family

Africans, I was told that there was a thick file at the South African consulate in Texas of all my activities, including the demonstrations, the cultural boycotts, and listings of my travels around the US. In addition, there were statements I'd made when testifying before the Georgia State Legislature in favor of disinvestment and in which I shared why I left South Africa. It seemed they had just about everything on my activities. Yet, after some struggle, they never gave me a visa but did instead give me a document that allowed me to enter South Africa and return to the States. I did come back in one piece to the US.

1990 – As a guest at the Namibian Independence Celebrations on March 21, this was the first opportunity to see Nelson Mandela after his release, followed by a visit to South Africa to consult with Nelson and other leaders.

1991 – The nature of this visit home was historical: it was the first Annual Conference of the ANC inside the country since its banning in 1960.

1992 – I accompanied an AFSC six-member fact-finding team to study and report on destabilizing violence occurring in South Africa. This led to the publication of *Politics of Hope and Fear: South Africa in Transition, November 1992.*

1994 – My next visit was in 1994 to observe and vote in the first democratic elections in Africa and attend the inauguration of Nelson Mandela.

1995 - One more visit home before returning permanently was a sabbatical of several months with the opportunity to observe and report to colleagues in the US on the highly charged November 1st local elections for municipal mayors and councils.

1996 – I returned home to live.

15

Returning Home to Vote, the Inauguration of Nelson Mandela, 1994

South Africa Elections

The 1994 elections in South Africa were to be held April 24-29. I joined a delegation of men and women who departed from the Atlanta Airport as international observers to observe the fairness and freeness of the elections. We were part of a larger group of 200 US Election Observers under the auspices of the Lawyers' Committee for Civil Rights Under the Law. There was excitement. It was an enormous responsibility to assist in the process that would decide whether the elections were valid or invalid. Our group was majority African American, for whom it was an emotional time and, for many, their very first visit to Africa.

My program report provided details:

> In preparation for this, the Program organized a group that would travel to South Africa as Observers for the elections. This required rapid information dissemination and constant contact with the Lawyers Committee to stay on top of qualifications and the organizing of travel documents. There were many fundraising events to make this observer trip a success. Many letters were sent out to businesses requesting their assistance with this project.
>
> For South Africans voting in this country, this Program was the liaison with the community group and the NAACP to ensure that as many South Africans as possible received voter education. This Program was successful in coordinating the televideo conference done by the NAACP, which South African voters, monitors, and observers were able to attend at Georgia State Univer-

sity. We were also the base for most media questions regarding voting in our area which led to the event at Georgia State University being publicized in the Atlanta Constitution. We were listed as the reference for information regarding this project.

Through Concerned Black Clergy there was the promotion and the dissemination of information regarding "Ten Day Countdown to Democracy." This was a vigil that marked each day with a prayer beginning ten days before the elections. This was used by Earl Shinholster the National Field Secretary for the NAACP to promote citizen awareness while doing his work to organize voter education in the United States.

For me, there was the particular tension in anticipation of observing the elections in KwaZulu (later in 1994 KwaZulu-Natal) and in Durban, where the Inkatha Freedom Party (IFP/Inkatha) had been reluctant to endorse the election. Here, probably more than in any other part of the country, the political situation remained fraught with the threatened electoral boycott. One's presence in Natal risked the threats of violence and loss of life. Until the last minute it appeared as though IFP would not participate in voting.

But I went to KwaZulu because that is where I was born, and where my family lives, and there I could share the day with my ninety-year-old mother, who voted from her wheelchair. Though separated, due to different assigned polling stations, she cast her vote, and I cast mine. My daughter, Nomhle, of the third generation in our family, cast her vote in Johannesburg.

This was a special moment for me, a moment I thought I would never ever live to see. It was a powerful, emotional moment—a final, crowning achievement of liberation.

Heather Gray and Thandi
Johannesburg, 1994 Elections
Permission of Heather Gray Collection

Inauguration of Nelson Mandela

At the inauguration of Nelson Mandela in Pretoria ten days after the election, I sat with my mother, absorbed in the excitement of the hour and this moment in my life. The thought that ran constantly through my mind was of my father and how he must be smiling in heaven watching what was happening at the inauguration. If he had lived, he would have been a very old man, almost one hundred years old.

Excerpt from My Report Presented at the Quaker Meeting House Upon My Return from Voting in South Africa (Appendix E)

A free South Africa also means an end of isolation, in that South Africa has been re-admitted into the family of nations.

It means not only the end of the worst form of racism in our century, but most significantly, the end of colonialism in Africa.

It means an end to the destabilization, the devastation and forced poverty upon the people of southern Africa as in Namibia, Angola, Mozambique, Zambia, and others who had been dominated by the system of South African apartheid system for too long. It means that the world will stop referring to South Africa in negative terms such as "the evil, the wicked system, the immoral, the repugnant" - and the one that I didn't say that de Klerk hated the most is 'the regime.'

This change in Africa also symbolizes the ushering in of a new nation with the prospects of peace and recovery for many millions of people in the region and has the potential of exacting a positive influence on African affairs, because much of Africa has been marginalized for too long.

As a South African, thank you for your support all these many years. And I look forward to seeing you in the next South African election in 1999.

Thandi Gcabashe, May 1994

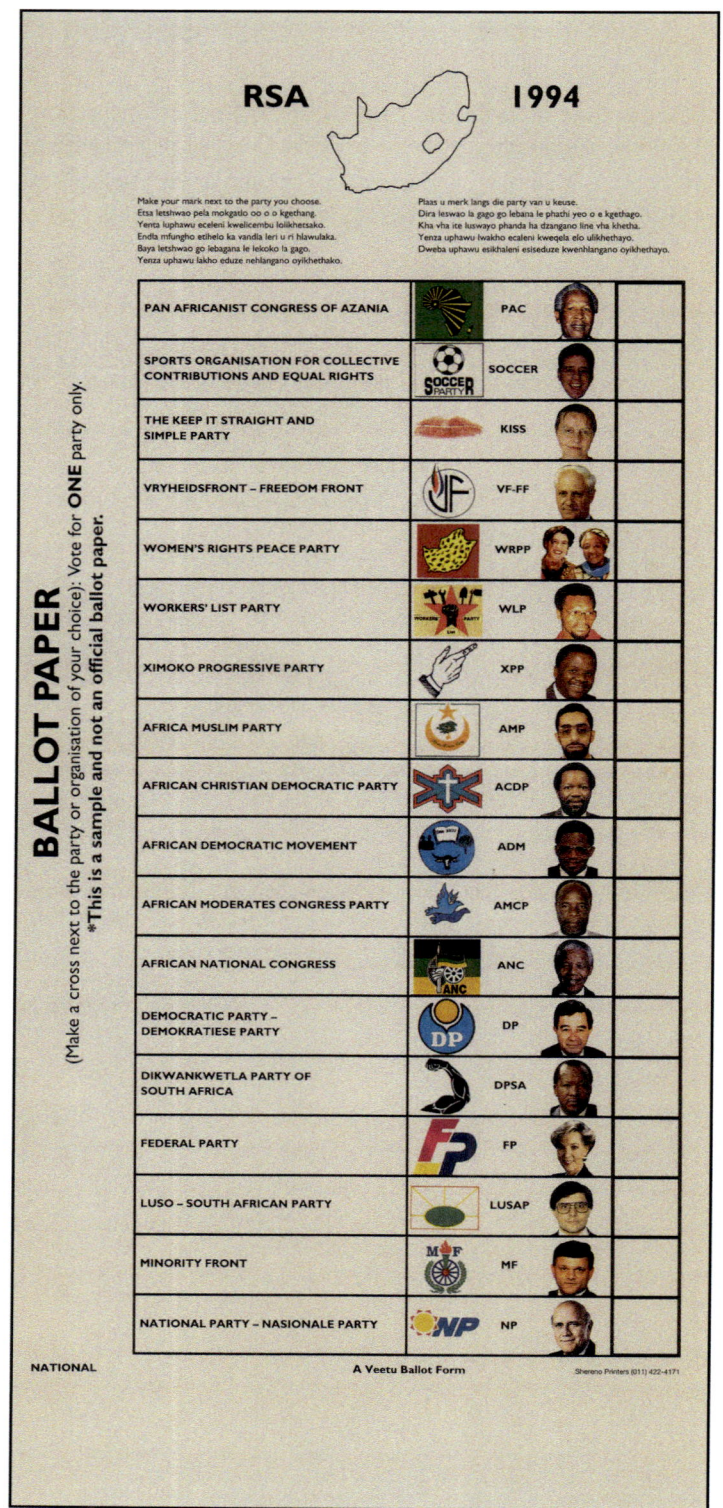

1994 South Africa Elections Sample Ballot Paper

Afterword

My feelings are strong that the international community's broad sanctions and divestments contributed significantly to the years of negotiation, the ultimate peaceful settlement, and the end of formalized apartheid. Our great task thereafter was the equally formidable challenge of nation-building. This we faced in a country whose people had great need and exultant expectations, where liberation movements were now responsible to govern equitably and deliver after decades of atrocities and intolerable poverty, when the energy of the anti-apartheid movement waned, the attention of the international community altered, and where the beauties and pitfalls of democracy were unknown and unpracticed.

There is no doubt in my mind that each of my parents contributed to the work I undertook in Atlanta and in the United States as a whole. They endowed me with values which are deeply embedded in who I am. My mother's great lessons of life, combined with my father's impeccable example of public service and total commitment to a cause, characterized the manner in which I applied myself to my own life's work.

In retrospect, I knew the decision to leave South Africa when we did was well considered. It removed my family from all but certain harm. I was able to deliver my children safely into adulthood. While I would have wanted a storybook life for them, I am convinced that no such thing exists. I believe that what I could give them was what my parents gave me, a strong sense of themselves, the freedom to determine their own destiny, and a fighting spirit.

My younger three children repatriated to South Africa beginning in 1991 with my second daughter, Nomhle, and my third daughter, Nokukhanya, in 1998. Both have families of their own. My son, Phakamele, returned in 2007. My oldest daughter, Sibongile, remains living in Atlanta today with her family. I returned from exile to South Africa permanently in 1996. The feelings were mixed upon my departure from Atlanta—sadness that I was leaving so many friends, especially in Atlanta, and joy to be returning at last to my home. We are a transcontinental family and remain close—my children close to each other and to me. There have been visits back and forth.

I am grateful to have been able to join the Department of Foreign Affairs in 1998 and continue my service to the people of South Africa as Ambassador to Venezuela,

Columbia, Ecuador, and the West Indies. These were interesting years for which another chapter could be written.

Taking a panoramic view of my life over the past eight decades, there was much doubt at several points along the way that I would ever experience the delight and hope that my grandchildren and great-grandchildren bring to me. Today, I can say without doubt that fighting to overcome and survive the travails of apartheid was worth every moment, just to be a grandmother. I thank God.

My grandchildren's world is substantially different than that of my childhood in the Groutville Mission Station during the 1930s and 1940s and I still worry that they will, indeed, face instances in their lives when the color of their skin will suppress in some way the realization of their fullest potential. It is painful for me to think of the futures of the hundreds of thousands of South African children who live under far more difficult circumstances than my grandchildren. While many have made incremental gains, their lives in many ways are more difficult than mine 70 years ago growing up in the generational ancestral birthplace of my father.

I hold the youth of our country and our world in my prayers. Always I have taken a keen interest in young people. I've spent much of my working time with students at all levels. While I have much to say and share and debate, I mostly wish to listen.

Annexes

Annex A
Tributes to Thandi

To Tandi
By Heather Gray

There's the smile, the gleam in her eye,
a tease about something or other and…
Suddenly you are hers, of her family.
The generosity, beauty, wisdom and
humility are Tandi, but more than that…
It is the richness of her African soul that has
Profoundly touched her countless
brothers and sisters on both continents.
Twenty-four years in exile.
The painful separation from loved ones,
Her own personal struggles, and yet…
The commitment, the dreams, the hard work,
the valiant and forthright call for justice,
the uncanny ability to unselfishly calm and
elevate the souls of those she has taken under her wing are constant.
With her very presence she has inspired us in the quest to
understand, to analyze and to never, never waiver in the
struggle for and with those treated unjustly.
As our mentor and learned teacher she has drawn us to Africa.
Tandi, we are honored to hold your hand in the land of your
ancestors. This moment, this day, this year are yours and that of your people.
We love you and thank you for allowing us the privilege of
sharing this unprecedented historical moment with you.

Written and read to Tandi at a dinner on
20 April 1994 Johannesburg, South Africa
preceding the first democratic elections in South Africa.

Let the work she has done speak for her
By Carol Luther

From the first to the last, one of the most memorable features of my work with Tandi was our road trips. By far, our first trip to Birmingham was both the best and the worst. Some say that traveling with a person is one of the true tests of your relationship, yet Tandi stands out among my friends and family with whom I have shared travel experiences, as a person that I could and will travel with without hesitation.

Soon after I moved to Atlanta from Philadelphia, friends suggested that I contact the AFSC Southeast Regional Office (SERO) for potential job opportunities. This was partly because I was the only person they knew with a degree in international affairs and partly because some of them worked in the AFSC National Office's Peace Division. Even though I had moved to Georgia to take a job at the University of Georgia, Athens, GA, its environs were such a cultural stretch for me that I left my position at the university voluntarily. Since I had not secured housing in Athens, this was an easy decision because it eliminated my daily 150-mile commute.

Betty Ligon, Tandi's SERO supervisor, was instrumental in convincing me to volunteer to help her expand her fledging Peace Education Program. I had been involved in the U.S. civil rights movement since 2nd grade in Memphis, TN, along with both my parents. Despite this, I had little direct knowledge of the international rights movement until the summer that I graduated high school. My freshman orientation package from Lincoln University, which included a copy of "Cry the Beloved Country," was my introduction to the ongoing struggle in South Africa. On a campus with a student population from throughout the African Diaspora, the world struggle against oppressive governments was part of my daily education. But as a student, one of my favorite professors, Alfred Moleah, a South African refugee, was a major influence in my development as a Pan-Africanist and anti-apartheid activist.

Since I was a native of the region, Tandi corralled me into making the first of many Peace Education tours through the Southeast, a joint activity of the AFSC national and SERO offices. Led by Jerry Herman and Tandi, we were an eclectic caravan of staff and activists that included an Englishman on his first trip to the Black Belt south. Strangely, our first contact point in Birmingham was an Hispanic family, activists in the local workers' rights movement. The wife welcomed us with a savory breakfast, the best coffee I have ever had, and a place to rest before heading out to find our contacts in the hometown of Evelyn Lowery and Coretta Scott King.

We've gone too far! As the co-pilot of the second car in our caravan, my unease grew as darkness descended on the narrow two-lane highway. Our directions for finding this town were somewhat limited to the distance from Birmingham and not much else that would prove useful. We sped up and flashed our headlights to catch the lead car and express our concern (no cell phones in early 1980s). Agreed that we should turn around, we passed the town again, then after reversing direction again, someone realized that we had passed a tiny flashing yellow light above the road for the third time. One last course correction, making a turn at that light, took us into the tiny town center, where we soon found the high school gym. Inside, having waited more than an hour, were field hands, school teachers and the local SCLC organizer, worried but relieved and ready to offer to help Tandi and her entourage defeat apartheid.

By the time we met Reverend Arrington, a Birmingham Baptist minister, who washed all of our feet, took up a collection, and prayed for traveling mercies for our group, it was clear that Tandi was gravely ill. She had mentioned a persistent unusual headache, but didn't complain or cancel any of our speaking engagements. Against her wishes, Jerry Herman, decided that Tandi should return to Atlanta, dispatching me and the Englishman with instructions to get her home. By the time we arrived, she could barely sit up and could hardly see. The next day, I learned that her family's decision to make her go to Grady Hospital was a major factor in her recovery from an impending neurological disaster.

Many of our subsequent road trips throughout the Southeast were less eventful, though some were equally arduous. We often stayed with Friends from local meeting houses or in the cheapest digs in town (that the SERO budget would allow). Sometimes we had no heat, sometimes our "contacts" were vociferously opposed to certain activities of the Peace Education Program. Some of the food that our hosts supplied us with was unfamiliar and disagreeable. And many more times, we got lost on our way to meet our supporters. But Tandi never complained, and more importantly, she never lost her way. She never wavered from her mission or message, even when faced with the tortuous Quaker process of finding consensus.

After I served as Tandi's Peace Education Committee chairperson for several years, she requested that I accept a position on the AFSC's national Peace Committee. While she offered no explanation, none was needed. Decisions made at AFSC' national office—from budget allocations to devolving (laying down) program activities to and policy positions—had far-reaching effects throughout the organization.

Just before the 1994 election in South Africa, an AFSC National Peace Education Committee meeting was the scene of one of my last road trips with Tandi. Because of the escalating violence in South Africa and the activities of certain political parties, the Committee had to decide whether to continue the organization's public policy in support of the transition to majority rule in South Africa. Withdrawing AFSC support would mean that Tandi's work would be severely restricted and possibly defunded.

After a full weekend of discussion (and pleading), the National Southern Africa Program Coordinator, Jerry Herman, was our sole impediment to arriving at consensus for a policy that would continue AFSC's support. Repeatedly he said, "They are not ready. We could be supporting a bloodbath, or worse." Both Tandi and I were shocked and bemused by Jerry's argument and his unceasing opposition to consensus that would let us move forward. Even the unflappable Tandi had run out of counter arguments that might sway Jerry.

Trapped between my two longtime friends, both with valid points on the table for consideration, I suddenly remembered how my journey to end apartheid had started. "This is their struggle, and it always has been," I said, and continued: "From the time I became aware, many have asked me to help, but not one South African ever asked me to tell them how to fight. They might not be ready, and they might make mistakes, but we simply don't have the right to second guess or lead this movement. Doing it now says to the world that AFSC never really supported the goal of this struggle. Let's eschew the violence as AFSC must but continue to champion the people of South Africa and the end of apartheid." When my longtime travel companion squeezed my hand, I knew that when we asked, Jerry would stand down, and that last road trip together would really be the best one ever.

Clerk, AFSC Southern Africa Program Committee, Atlanta, GA
Member, AFSC National Peace Education Committee, Philadelphia, PA

Ode to Thandi Gcabashe
by Dr. Mack H. Jones

Beginning in the late 1960s, students and faculty of Atlanta University, particularly the Political Science Department, became integral elements in the national and international struggle for African liberation. Students and faculty created local support groups to build greater awareness of the extent and nature of racial oppression in various African countries as a prelude to mobilizing and organizing the people for transformative action. The groups were keenly interested in supporting those involved in armed struggle in what was then Namibia, Rhodesia, Angola, and Mozambique and later South Africa. Students and faculty conducted forums and workshops on and off campus, solicited participation of existing civil rights and community organizations and influential personalities, and collected funds and other resources that were made available to liberation movements. When sister Thandi Gcabashe and her husband, Thulani, came to Atlanta as revolutionaries in exile they were welcomed by what was then an active and growing support movement.

Thandi and Thulani quickly became valued pillars in the African liberation support movement not only in Atlanta and the Southeastern United States but throughout the country. A tireless worker and effective speaker, Thandi spent countless hours and traveled many miles in the region explaining the nature of the apartheid state and the complicity of the West and the United States in particular in aiding and abetting the South African regime. She got to know and conducted discussions with scores of prominent Atlanta leaders, both Blacks and whites, many of whom she persuaded to become allies in the struggle to end the apartheid regime.

The struggle to persuade or force companies to withdraw investments from South Africa as a way to cripple the regime economically was a priority for Thandi and the Atlanta African liberation movement. Coca-Cola, one of the world's most visible companies and head quartered in Atlanta was a prime target of the divestment program. If Coke was forced to divest that would be a watershed development in the movement. However, most Atlanta leaders and institutions were beholden to Coke for one reason or another and were reluctant to publicly challenge the company. Having shown considerable skills as a conciliator, Thandi was not deterred by the lukewarm support offered by Atlanta leaders. She cobbled together a coalition of academics, churches, and other community organizations and conducted a sustained campaign that forced Coke to relent.

The divestment campaign was a key element in bringing down the apartheid regime and the Coke boycott as a seminal moment in the divestment campaign and Thandi was key to making it happen. The heroines and heroes in the struggle to end the apartheid regime may be too numerous to count but a central place will always be reserved for Thandi.

Professor Emeritus, Clark University, Atlanta, GA
1st President, National Conference of Black Political Scientists (NCOBPS)
Former Chair, Political Science Department, Atlanta University

Thandi and her Influence in Atlanta
by Dr. Earl Picard

I came to graduate school in Atlanta in 1973 after participating in African Liberation Day activities in New Orleans, attending the African Liberation Support Committee (ALSC) meeting in Frogmore, S.C., and spending a summer in West Africa.

I entered graduate school in the midst of a personal period of student, community, and anti-colonial activism. Africa was very much a part of my consciousness and recent experience, and I was eager to build on that as I entered graduate school. I was not disappointed.

I found any number of kindred souls from activist backgrounds at Atlanta University who were grounded scholars, voracious learners and committed activists for African liberation. The Political Science Department provided a diet of Fanon, DuBois, Nkrumah, Nyerere, Mandela and Cabral. We had courses on Africa's politics, political economy, and international relations. We had a course on Southern Africa which helped us to match our intellectual development with our activism against white minority rule and Portuguese colonialism.

We formed an Atlanta chapter of ALSC and supported the African liberation movements in Zimbabwe, South Africa, Namibia, and the former Portuguese colonies. We supported the movement to boycott Gulf Oil. We organized forums and demonstrations, handed out leaflets on the streets of Atlanta, and raised funds as we could. There were others who focused on African liberation issues, and we worked with them to broaden impact. I remember, particularly, the demonstration we organized to protest Ray Charles' visit to Sun City in contravention of the boycott of South Africa. That was a painful moment since he was, for most of us, an icon. We also were closely involved with the effort to get M&M Products, the Atlanta based black owned hair care company, to divest from South Africa.

We did all that while being full-time, focused graduate students and faculty in a very demanding program. We had other commitments and fit our liberation support activities into our already crowded lives and days. We were not full-time.

When Thandi came to head the Southern Africa Program at the AFSC we had a person who worked full time at the task. She became a focal point, an information channel, a catalyst. She'd see to it that someone got to a forum or meeting to speak, or make a radio interview, if the opportunity presented itself. She worked to get the story out, feeling that if people just had accurate information they would be sympathetic. She brought people together around that belief.

My fondest memories come after the elections in South Africa and after Thandi had gone home to Durban. I took a job in South Africa in 1997 and reconnected with her. In 1998 Mack Jones briefly joined me in South Africa to interview prospective students for one of our scholarship programs. We had interviews in several cities, including Durban, and made sure to let Thandi know we would be in her city. She came to the hotel and spent a wonderful afternoon with us. We were so joyous. I felt it was a deep celebration for things unspoken. We had seen our spirits lifted and our sometimes lonely efforts confirmed, and here we were in a free South Africa.

I also fondly remember Nomhle's wedding in Durban. I knew few people other than the Gcabashes, but I was invited, and I went and had a great time. It was so immersive, so authentic. I felt I had found my way into the culture. I've always loved when I find myself in a profoundly organic moment in the lives of the people I am among. That's the way I felt about the wedding. It remains one of my fondest memories of South Africa.

My final memories are from watching Thandi become Ambassador Gcabashe. I lived in Pretoria which was where the diplomatic training center was located. Thandi had to move to Pretoria when she was preparing for her Ambassadorship. The center was very accessible for me, and I visited her there. When Thandi was named Ambassador, I was one of her guests at dinner with the Venezuelan Ambassador. I was proud to know that Thandi's character, steadfastness and focus had brought her to this point. It was a fitting reward for all her efforts and sacrifice.

Senior Research Associate and Director of Strategic Planning and Development, Office of International Initiatives, Georgia State University, Atlanta, GA (Retired)
Graduate Faculty Member for Comparative and Africa Politics, Atlanta University
Representative in Zimbabwe and in South Africa, Institute of International Education

Reflections on Thandi Gcabashe
by Elizabeth Enloe

The lights often burned late into the nights during the 1980s in the American Friends Service Committee's downtown Atlanta office at the corner of Piedmont Avenue and Houston Street. It was obvious then, and even more so now upon reflection, how this simple two-story building, just blocks from the heart of Sweet Auburn and Dr. King's legacy, provided a haven to many activists for justice to meet, discuss, and organize. It was a welcoming space filled with intensity, compassion, awakenings, and laughter. Thandi shared these offices and the large meeting space with AFSC colleagues working on the Middle East conflict, peace and disarmament, and the many programs and activities hosted by the AFSC to which so many volunteers came to join Thandi in anti-apartheid initiatives.

Thandi was established in her role as program director for the Southern Africa Peace Education Program when I arrived in 1983. To my knowledge she never imposed on me the stereotypes of the white woman from the North, appointed to direct the AFSC's programs in the Southeast. Though technically her supervisor, the relationship over the years evolved into a partnership with, I hope, few administrative burdens on Thandi. Her accomplishments overrode the consistent strains of insufficient funding. There were occasional sensitive moments for me: entering our volunteer filled conference room to address the elusive "we" and delicate balance between Thandi's role with the AFSC and the Georgia Coalition for Divestment in South Africa. Similarly, before the eventual call for the *Coca-Cola Boycott,* I needed to convince many ready individuals that a pause for further dialogue with Coke would be in the best interests of success. Fortunately, Thandi and I agreed. Had we more time for in-depth conversations it would have been wonderful, yet we covered the essentials.

On May 17, 2015, I presented Thandi to receive the honorary degree of Doctor of Humane Letters from Haverford College with words as heartfelt then as they are now:

> …we can name individuals of principle and courage and heroic proportions - Albert Luthuli, Nelson Mandela, Nadine Gordimer, Alan Paton, Walter Sisulu, Helen Suzman, Leah and Desmond Tutu - who challenged apartheid's vicious laws and achieved emancipation from apartheid's bondage for all – white and black. Among these individuals is Thandeka Luthuli Gcabashe.

> Those of us privileged to work with Thandi, witnessed a gracious, compassionate, strong-as-steel woman emerge as a supremely influential activist. The daughter of Nokukhanya and Albert Luthuli, few if any were better prepared to illuminate the structural horror of apartheid and its human impact, and navigate the landscape of conflicted political alliances. As analyst, negotiator, mediator, Thandi became central to the anti-apartheid organizations and movement in this country. As a gifted organizer, she galvanized disparate

groups for the greater good. She led divestment campaigns and boycotts. With little financial support, she became immune to the rigors of vigils, protests, speaking engagements, late hours and miles and miles of travel. And, if exhaustion set in, she found new reserves. Humble beyond words she discomfited powerful individuals and corporations with truth. She was willing to be the thorn in someone's side while gently persuading them to think anew. Agile and at home with a wide range of people, her grassroots and national work is reflected in countless campus newspapers, and small church bulletins, and photographs on impressive stages with renowned individuals. That her work was headquartered in the South was no coincidental matter. Thandi has been honored and given keys to many of its small towns and great cities.

During the president's reception dinner, the students gravitated to Thandi. When most guests had departed, around her was an engaged group that could have continued talking well into the night. It was emblematic of her empathy and interest in young people.

Thandi's completion of her "Liberation" memoir is a gift to us all. She calls us to be uncomfortable with the past from which it is easy to distance oneself. Her words reveal similarities with what came before and what is happening now. With quiet language she references monumental world events—colonialization and liberation movements, the UN's founding and *Declaration of Human Rights*, the Cold War politics of communism, and the similarities between US Jim Crow and South Africa apartheid laws. She introduces many of her life's threads—the atrocities of human cruelty, the essential careers of teaching and nursing, the role of faith, the bonds of family, the rightly placed passions of youth, women as game changers, and the morality of disruptive actions. Each thread has its own historical context, yet each connects to current realities—voter suppression, slavery and segregation, the disparities between the highest standards of living and lowest, and the example of sacrifice and perseverance.

"Liberation" invites us to recognize the life struggles of those who witnessed wrongs and were determined to fight for human dignity and equality. It makes possible what is richly deserved, an historical and personal record of a woman whose life's work belongs in the pantheon of individuals who envisioned and helped make possible a multiracial South Africa.

Former Regional Director, Southeast (Atlanta) and New York Metropolitan Regional Offices, American Friends Service Committee
Former Manager, Board of Managers, Haverford College, Haverford, PA

Annex B
Awards and Recognitions

Thandeka (Thandi) Luthuli Gcabashe

2018 – July 26
USA House of Representatives, Read into the Congressional Record,
Vol. 164, No. 126 by Sanford D. Bishop, Jr. of Georgia
"Recognizing Former Ambassador Thandeka Luthuli-Gcabashe"
Washington, DC

RECOGNIZING FORMER AMBASSADOR THANDEKA LUTHULI-GCABASHE

HON. SANFORD D. BISHOP, JR.
of Georgia
in the house of representatives
Thursday, July 26, 2018

Mr. BISHOP of Georgia. Mr. Speaker, I rise today to pay tribute to an inspiring activist, dedicated servant for mankind, and former South African Ambassador to the Caribbean, Thandeka (Thandi) Luthuli Gcabashe. Ambassador Gcabashe will be in Albany, Georgia this week and it is my honor and pleasure to welcome her to the Second Congressional District of Georgia where she will be visiting her friend of longstanding, Dougherty County Commissioner, Gloria Gaines.

Thandeka, also known as Thandi, is one of two daughters born to Chief Albert Luthuli and Nokukhanya Bhengu. Chief Luthuli was Nelson Mandela's predecessor in the African National Congress where he served as President from 1952-1967. He was also the second black man to win the Nobel Peace Prize for his nonviolent approach to fighting South Africa's Apartheid.

Throughout her life, Ambassador Gcabashe continued to uphold her father's dedication to peace and human rights through her work in South Africa and the United States of America. While in South Africa, she coordinated South Africa's Peace Education Program and lectured to civic, cultural, and educational institutions on the pressing issues surrounding Apartheid. In 1970, shortly after the death of her father, she fled South Africa with her husband and four children, and they settled in Atlanta, Georgia with the help of the American Embassy and the late activist, Mrs. Caretta Scott-King. While in the U.S., she continued to condemn the Apartheid and played a pivotal role in coordinating the American response. She returned to South Africa in 1996, following the end of Apartheid. She went on to join South Africa's Department of Foreign Affairs in 1998 and in 1999 was appointed Ambassador to Venezuela, Latin America, and the West Indies (the Caribbean).

Former Ambassador Gcabashe's work has earned her numerous awards and accolades such as the ONI Award from the International Black Women's Congress, the Civil Liberation Award from the Civil Liberties Union of Georgia, and an honorary Doctorate from Haverford College.

Nelson Mandela said, ``A good head and a good heart are always a formidable combination.'' Ambassador Gcabashe undoubtedly possesses this combination and the evidence is noted in her distinguished service to her country, devotion to her work, and the compassion she has shown for the people of the Caribbean.

Mr. Speaker, I ask my colleagues to join me today in recognizing former South African Ambassador, Thandeka (Thandi) Luthuli Gcabashe. The Second Congressional

> District of Georgia welcomes this outstanding woman and
> applauds her dedication and service to the betterment of
> mankind.

2015 – May 17
Honorary Degree, Doctor of Humane Letters, honoris causa
Haverford College, Haverford, Pennsylvania

2013 – February 21
Acceptance of a resolution commending Chief Albert John Luthuli and **recognizing February 21, 2013, as Chief Albert Luthuli Day at the Georgia State Capitol**;
Proclamation naming **Thandi an Honorary Citizen of Georgia and Goodwill Ambassador**;
Distinction of **Honorary Membership in the Georgia Legislative Black Caucus**; and
Keys to the City of Dalton, GA given to her by the Mayor, David Pennington.

Multiple friends and admirers welcomed Thandi Luthuli Gcabashe back to the United States during her February 2013 visit to Atlanta, Georgia. Daughter of the Nobel Peace Prize winner (1960) and the African National Congress President, Chief Albert Luthuli, Thandi was a key figure in the movement to end apartheid, both in South Africa and the US. As a political exile during the last decades of the apartheid regime, Thandi and her family settled in Atlanta, GA. In 1981 she was appointed Director of the American Friends Service Committee's Southern Africa Peace Education Program, a post she occupied for 15 years.

Thandi returned to Johannesburg in 1994 to vote in the first post-apartheid election. Under the Nelson Mandela presidency she served as South African Ambassador to Venezuela. She currently lives in Durban.

Able to work with persons across political and social spectrums, Thandi was a nationwide leader, crisscrossing the Southeast and the country to speak to audiences large and small. She initiated multiple education projects and divestment campaigns. She tirelessly gave of herself and earned the respect of all who met her.

Thandi's 2013 speaking tour to the US was prompted by the re-publication of the autobiography of Albert Luthuli. Addressing audiences at the Georgia State Capital, on college campuses and at community forums and radio shows, she provided insight into South African during the most recent presidencies.

Thandi graciously accepted a resolution commending Chief Albert John Luthuli and recognizing February 21, 2013, as Chief Albert Luthuli Day at the Georgia State Capitol; a proclamation naming Thandi an Honorary Citizen of Georgia and Goodwill Ambassador; the distinction of Honorary Membership in the Georgia Legislative Black Caucus; and Keys to the City of Dalton, GA given to her by the Mayor, David Pennington.

1995 – February 16
National Association of Black Women in Government (NABWG) tribute to the four Black Nobel Peace Prize Winners
Washington, DC

1994 – May 21
Tandi Luthuli Gcabashe Day
Proclamation by Bill Campbell,
Mayor of the City of Atlanta, Georgia

1991 – November 17-18
Honored guest at event launching **Luthuli-Mandela Lecture Series**
Project of Fisk University and Meharry Medical College
Nashville, Tennessee

1990 – May
Fourth Annual Law Day Luncheon "Generations of Justice"
Minority Bar Liaison Committee of the Atlanta Council of Younger Lawyers
Appreciation of Tandi Luthuli Gcabashe

1990 – May 19
Civic Liberties Award
Serene Lodge 567-20th Century Temple 656 IBPO Elks of the World
Atlanta, Georgia

1989 – December 8
Civil Libertarian Award
American Civil Liberties Union of Georgia
Presented to Tandi Luthuli Gcabashe, Dedicated to the Anti-Apartheid Movement to Free South Africa. To Honor You for Dreaming the Dream, Sharing the Vision, and Making it Happen.
Atlanta, Georgia

1988
African Woman Activist Award
African Women's Center, Atlanta University
Atlanta, Georgia

1985
ONI Award
International Black Women's Congress for commitment to uplifting lives of people of African descent
Atlanta, Georgia

1985 – September 28
Africa Woman Activist Award
Africa Women's Center, Atlanta University
Atlanta, Georgia

1984
Metro Atlanta Kwanza Award
Metro Atlanta Kwanza Association
Atlanta, Georgia

Appendices

Appendix A

Appeal for Action Against Apartheid
Joint statement by Chief Albert J. Luthuli and Reverend Dr. Martin Luther King, Jr.
December 10, 1962

In 1957, an unprecedented Declaration of Conscience was issued by more than 100 leaders from every continent. That Declaration was an appeal to South Africa to bring its policies into line with the Universal Declaration of Human Rights adopted by the General Assembly of the United Nations.

The Declaration was a good start in mobilising world sentiment to back those in South Africa who acted for equality. The non-whites took heart in learning that they were not alone. And many white supremacists learned for the first time how isolated they were.

Measures of Desperation

Subsequent to the Declaration, the South African Government took the following measures:

BANNED the African National Congress and the Pan Africanist Congress, the principal protest organisations, and jailed their leaders;

COERCED the press into strict pro-government censorship and made it almost impossible for new anti-apartheid publications to exist;

ESTABLISHED an arms industry, more than tripled the military budget, distributed small arms to the white population, enlarged the army, created an extensive white civilian militia;

ACTIVATED total physical race separation by establishing the first Bantustan in the Transkei - with the aid of emergency police regulations;

LEGALLY DEFINED protest against apartheid as an act of "sabotage" - an offence ultimately punishable by death;

PERPETUATED its control through terrorism and violence:
- Human Rights Day (December 10), 1959 - 12 South West Africans killed at Windhoek and 40 wounded as they fled police

- March 21, 1960 - 72 Africans killed and 186 wounded at Sharpeville by police
- Before and during the two-year "emergency" in the Transkei - 15 Africans killed by police, thousands arrested and imprisoned without trial.

The Choice

The deepening tensions can lead to two alternatives:

Solution 1

Intensified persecution may lead to violence and armed rebellion once it is clear that peaceful adjustments are no longer possible. As the persecution has been inflicted by one racial group upon all other racial groups, large-scale violence would take the form of a racial war.

This "solution" may be workable. But mass racial extermination will destroy the potential for interracial unity in South Africa and elsewhere.

Therefore, we ask for your action to make the following possible:

Solution 2

"Nothing which we have suffered at the hands of the government has turned us from our chosen path of disciplined resistance," said Chief Albert J. Lutuli at Oslo. So there exists another alternative - and the only solution which represents sanity - transition to a society based upon equality for all without regard to colour.

Any solution founded on justice is unattainable until the Government of South Africa is forced by pressures, both internal and external, to come to terms with the demands of the non-white majority.

The apartheid republic is a reality today only because the peoples and governments of the world have been unwilling to place her in quarantine.

Translate public opinion into public action.

We, therefore, ask all men of goodwill to take action against apartheid in the following manner:

- Hold meetings and demonstrations on December 10, Human Rights Day;
- Urge your church, union, lodge, or club to observe this day as one of protest;
- Urge your Government to support economic sanctions;
- Write to your mission to the United Nations urging adoption of a resolution calling for international isolation of South Africa;
- Don't buy South Africa's products;

- Don't trade or invest in South Africa;
- Translate public opinion into public action by explaining facts to all peoples, to groups to which you belong, and to countries of which you are citizens until AN EFFECTIVE INTERNATIONAL QUARANTINE OF APARTHEID IS ESTABLISHED.

This joint statement, initiated by Chief Lutuli and the Rev. Dr. Martin Luther King, Jr., was signed by many prominent Americans and promoted the public campaign for sanctions against South Africa.

Appendix B
AFSC History with Southern Africa, Highlights

1917   AFSC founded in Philadelphia during World War I to provide conscientious objectors with alternative work to military service.

1947   AFSC, with British Friends Service Council, awarded the Nobel Peace Prize for worldwide work of the Religious Society of Friends (Quakers).

Late 1950s & 1960s – AFSC begins organizational involvement in Africa, focused on Algerian war refugees, and South Africa freedom movement. Its program work in the US was shaped by growing awareness of oppression through connections with political freedom movements and strong personal ties with individuals in Central and Southern Africa through the visit of Douglas and Dorothy Steele; by George and Eleanor Loft posted in in Southern Rhodesia (Zimbabwe) in 1957 followed by Lyle and Bickie Tatum in 1960-1964; and by Jim and Christine Bristol as AFSC representatives in Zambia in 1965-1967.

1958   AFSC sponsors the visit to India for Martin Luther King, Jr. and Coretta Scott King to deepen connections with the nonviolent legacy of Mahatma Gandhi.

1961-1968 – AFSC's worldwide Voluntary International Service Assignments (VISA) provided two-year volunteer opportunities in Tanzania in health care, rural reconstruction, agriculture, and education projects.

1963   AFSC publishes Dr. Martin Luther King's *Letter from Birmingham City Jail*.

1965   AFSC begins South Africa divestment dialogue with Chase Manhattan Bank.

1969   AFSC closes Chase Manhattan Bank account in protest.

1970s – 1980s – AFSC becomes one of several major US organizations with anti-apartheid work. Its pacifist commitment remains steadfast while understanding African movements embrace of armed struggle. AFSC Offices throughout the US—Atlanta, St. Petersburg, Seattle, Portland, Baltimore, Ohio, Western Massachusetts, and North Carolina—become centers for local anti-apartheid work. Staff become fully involved in divestment movement, calling on universities, cities, states, and other institutions to withdraw investments from US companies involved in South Africa. AFSC National and Regional Offices support passage of Comprehensive Anti-Apartheid Act of 1986.

1972   In *Nonviolence Not First for Export,* Jim Bristol reflects that "I believe in nonviolent revolution, but I also believe that it is neither humane nor practical to urge nonviolent revolution upon others whose situation is so totally different from our own."

1975   AFSC hires Bill Sutherland as Quaker International Affairs Representative to establish the AFSC's Southern Africa Program with support of AFSC staff Lyle Tatum, Jim Bristol, Peter Molotsi, and Michael Simmons. Bill was based in both Dar es Salaam and the US, spending 6 months in the region and 6 months traveling in the US, educating Americans about apartheid and the liberation movements.

1976   AFSC distributes *Action Guide on South Africa.*

1977   AFSC undertakes study trip to Kenya, Zambia, Tanzania, Mozambique, and Botswana, led by Bill Sutherland, to meet with government leaders and members of liberation movements in exile. AFSC's recognizes southern part of the US as having fewer anti-apartheid groups. AFSC establishes Atlanta-based Southern Africa Program and begins support for only full-time staffed program in the southern part of the United States to address apartheid.

1978   *Southern Africa Summer* organized by Michael Simmons, AFSC Southern African Program Director in National Office, places college and high school students in 10 US cities to focus on ending bank loans to South Africa.

1979   Bishop Tutu visits AFSC National Office in Philadelphia 5 May 1979.

1980   AFSC underwrites study trip to South Africa, South Africa-occupied Namibia, Botswana, and Zimbabwe to continue dialogues particularly with South African Quakers with opposing views on economic sanctions. Participants meet with Desmond Tutu.

1980   Jerry Herman hired to lead the AFSC's national Southern Africa Program.

1981   Thandi Luthuli Gcabashe hired to direct AFSC's Atlanta-based Southern African Program for the southeastern region.

1981   AFSC national Southern African Program launches weeks-long,

Appendix B: AFSC History with Southern Africa, Highlights

multi-state US regional speaking tours to increase awareness of local communities through conversations with informed individuals from US anti-apartheid organizations and representatives of African liberation movements. AFSC is also a member of the coalition-supported, parallel Africa Peace Tours with similar purpose.

1982 AFSC formalizes policy position and publishes *South Africa: Challenge and Hope*. AFSC publishes *Automating Apartheid*, a study on the role of high-tech U.S. exports in reinforcing South Africa's military and security apparatus.

1981 & 1982 – AFSC nominates Desmond Tutu for Nobel Peace Prize. He is awarded the recognition in 1983.

1985 AFSC hosts Leah Tutu on US tour to speak in Philadelphia, Washington, DC, Atlanta, and Jackson, Mississippi.

1985 With the Georgia Coalition for Divestment in South Africa, AFSC launches and co-sponsors the Coca-Cola Campaign leading to the six-year *Boycott* of Coke products as part of worldwide divestment movement.

1987 AFSC National Office begins publication of *U.S. Anti-Apartheid Newsletter*.

1987 Africa Peace Tour focused on US southern states—Louisiana, Mississippi, Alabama, Georgia, Florida, South Carolina, and North Carolina—addressed apartheid and militarization of U.S. foreign and South Africa's wars on neighboring countries.

1992 AFSC sponsors fact-finding team to study violence in black townships, and publishes report, "Politics of Hope and Fear: South Africa in Transition."

1993 AFSC formally concludes *Coca-Cola Boycott* in anticipation of South Africa leadership request to end sanctions.

1994 AFSC sends observers to South Africa elections.

1994 and beyond – AFSC supports peace and reconciliation in Angola and Burundi, and promotes post-conflict demilitarization in Southern Africa. AFSC focuses on debt reduction and cancellation, on-going Africa Peace with Justice Educational Tours, and annual Bill Sutherland Institute for Africa advocates.

Excerpted from
American Friends Service Committee and Africa, Vision and Action Over Five Decades
By William Minter, Research by Matthew Baird, May 2021, and AFSC website

Thandi: Liberation

Appendix C
Thandi Gcabashe Speaking Engagements

1981 – 1994

Partial List
Engagements as keynote speaker, panel and forum participant, radio guest, conference and meeting participant, demonstration and rally speaker.
Events often represent multiple engagements.
Does not include reports to AFSC and GCDSA, articles, statements, and press releases.
Source: AFSC Reports, News Clippings

1981
Source: 9 Feb. 1982 Report to AFSC Executive Committee

1.	AFSC Southern Africa Peace Tour Southeast States AFSC, SWAPO, ANC, Defense and Aid Fund, Campaign to Oppose Bank Loans to South Africa, Washington Office on Africa	Nov.	
2.	Black Trade Unionist Coalition		Atlanta, GA
3.	Martin Luther King Center – *South Africa: Time Running Out*		Atlanta, GA
4.	Southern Africa Solidarity Conference		Berea, KY
5.	Emory University		Atlanta
6.	Georgia State		Atlanta
7.	"Heroes Day"	Dec. 16	Atlanta
8.	"Crossroads" 1st in series of human rights in SA	Dec.	Atlanta

1982
Source: 3 Feb. 1983 Program Report

9. Bill Sutherland's tour to activate constituents — Nov. 29-30 Atlanta

1983
Source: 4 1983 Minutes

10. "We've broken ground…" — Greensboro & Charlotte, NC; Jackson & Oxford, MI; New Orleans & Tallahassee, FL

Source: 6 Sept. 1983 Program Report

11. Divestment Conference – attended — Boston, MA
12. MLK, Jr. Center – series of lectures to summer interns — Atlanta
13. Presbyterian Church Conference – 2 weeks workshops, Educational activities, orientation of ministers to travel to SA — Atlanta

Source: 6 Sept. 1983 Minutes

14.	National Education Association (NEA Summer Conference speaker)	June 29	
15.	Oxford high school contacted		
16.	Atlanta University's "African Women's Summer Institute'	Summer	Atlanta
17.	20th Anniversary of March on Washington	27 August	Washington, DC
18.	New York University Student Conference on Divestment	7-9 Oct.	New York, NY
19.	Southeast Region Student Divestment Meeting	19 Nov.	Atlanta

1984

20.	Workshops, radio shows, and public addresses with Gloria Gaines	Sept.	Albany, GA
21.	Northwestern Lutheran Theological Seminary	Sept.	Minneapolis, MN
22.	18-member speaking tour	Sept.	Minnesota, No. Dakota, Wisconsin
23.	Student Divestment Conference, ITC	Oct.	Atlanta
24.	Speaking Tour, 4 teams, 26 cities, 9 states	7-14 Oct.	
25.	YMCA and AKA Sorority	21 Oct.	Atlanta
26.	Media events related to Bishop Tutu's winning Nobel Prize	26-27 Oct.	Atlanta
27.	Jomandi Productions of "Boseman and Lena" panel	26-27 Oct.	Atlanta
28.	Harper High School		Atlanta
29.	Wheeler High School		Atlanta
30.	Georgia State University		Atlanta
31.	Spelman College		Atlanta
32.	Morehouse College		Atlanta
33.	Presbyterian Center		Atlanta
34.	United Methodist Church		Atlanta
35.	3-day conference	16-18 Nov.	Montgomery, AL

1985

36.	Speaking Tour	April	Illinois
37.	Tuskegee Institute – sermon at Bernard Lafayette's church		Alabama
38.	First United Methodist Church - sermons	March	Griffin, GA
39.	Town Hall Meeting – City Hall		Atlanta, GA
40.	Morehouse College - 2000 students, Andrew Young, Julian Bond, John Lewis joined on podium by Thandi, and daughters of Bishop Tutu and MLK		Atlanta, GA
41.	National Student Conference on South Africa and Namibia	1-3 Nov.	New York NY,
42.	Morehouse Rally		
43.	Demonstrations at offices of Coca-Cola, General Motors, Westin Peachtree Plaza Hotel, Holiday Inn, IBM and the Georgia Stamp and Coin Shop	March/April 1985	Atlanta

Appendix C: Thandi Gcabashe Speaking Engagements

1986

Source: December 1985-February 1986 Program Report

44.	Savannah Divestment Group		Savannah, GA
45.	Mercer University		Macon, GA
46.	Lenoir-Rhyne College		Hickory, NC
47.	Amnesty International		Augusta, GA
48.	Community group		Tifton, GA
49.	Community group		Athens, GA
50.	Namibian Council Conference		Atlanta, GA
51.	International Black Women's Caucus		Atlanta, GA
52.	University of Tennessee –Campus Ministers & Amnesty International	Jan.	Knoxville, TN
53.	Black History month talks – churches and schools	Feb.	Georgia
54.	Delta Sigma Theta Sorority introducing apartheid curriculum to Atlanta Public Schools		Atlanta
55.	Thandi's home - Indian Community Removal from Big Mountain		

Source: 5-86 Program Report

56.	Spelman College with Mayor Andrew Young – Spelman divests!		Atlanta GA
57.	Fundraising for two anti-apartheid activists	April	Houston, TX
58.	Inter-Religious Conference for Economic Pressure against South Africa in New York – keynote	April	New York, NY
59.	North Decatur Presbyterian Church- month-long lecture series	April	Atlanta, GA
60.	Orlando City Council on divestment – decided on Sullivan Principles	May	Orlando, FL
61.	Africa Peace Tour – war and militarization in Africa 4-page list of speaking engagements	May	Atlanta & Miami Gainesville, FL
62.	Film Forum – "Palestine/South Africa" King Center with Themba Vilakazi of ANC and Mubarak Awad of Palestine Center for Nonviolence – Timothy McDonald facilitated	30 May	Atlanta, GA

8-1986 Program Report

63.	*Asinamali* – play from South Africa with South African performers		
64.	Bishop Manas Buthelezi of the Lutheran Church – press conference at Pascal's Guest speaker of AFSC, ITC, SCLC, Concerned Black Clergy		
65.	Soweto Day Conference		Toronto, Canada
66.	Humphries Elementary School		
67.	Atlanta Junior College	May	Atlanta, GA
68.	Forums with Bishop Farsami of the Lutheran Church at the invitation of Amnesty International	May	Atlanta, GA

69.	Thandi Interviews Prime Cable's Public Access channel, WRFG Radio, WSB Radio Atlanta Journal Constitution cable station	June	Atlanta. GA
70.	"Human Dignity in South Africa & at Home" forum MLK Center	13 June	Atlanta, GA
71.	"Solemn Meeting for Freedom in South Arica" Woodruff Library	15 June	Atlanta
72.	U.N. Council		Atlanta
73.	Interdenominational Theological Center		Atlanta
74.	Three-day conference		Arkansas
75.	"ONE PERSON/ONE VOTE" film forum Atlanta Night Talk Family and the Georgia Coalition for Divestment co-sponsored as a fundraiser for the Coke Campaign. Rick Reed, of the Atlanta Night Talk Family as moderator, Tandi Gcabashe, David Ndaba of the ANC, Makini Coleman	8 July	Atlanta, GA
76.	Samora Machel Memorial	31 Oct.	Atlanta

November -1986 report

77.	Speaking Engagement		Chattanooga, TN
78.	Speaking Engagement		Kentucky
79.	Spelman College		Atlanta, GA
80.	Agnes Scott College		Atlanta
81.	Morehouse College		Atlanta
82.	Fulton High School		Atlanta
83.	Wheeler High School		Atlanta
84.	North Cobb High School		Atlanta
85.	Archer High School		Atlanta
86.	Catholic Conference in Gwinnet County		Atlanta
87.	Ebenezer Baptist Church		Atlanta
88.	The Lawyers Guild		Atlanta
89.	Community Group		Gainesville, FL
90.	Georgia State University		Atlanta, GA
91.	Artists Against Apartheid – dance ensemble	15 Dec.	Atlanta

1987

Program Reports

92.	Divestment Legislation introduced on MLK Birthday Press Conference – State Capitol	15 Jan.	Atlanta
93.	"Let Your Voice Be Heard" – Central Presbyterian Church	29 Jan.	Atlanta
94.	Public Hearing		

February 1987 – Quarterly Report

95.	South Africa Awareness Week presentations with South African speakers and American experts. Clark College, Morehouse College, Atlanta Junior College, Georgia State University	7-22 Feb.	Atlanta

Appendix C: Thandi Gcabashe Speaking Engagements

from 4-page list of 1986-1987 events

96.	"Speak Truth to the People" Atlanta Videotape of ANC Pres. Tambo's speech made during Atlanta visit	25 Feb.	
97.	Atlanta Fulton County Library		Atlanta
98.	Amandala (Power!) Forum on South Africa – Clark College	26 Feb.	Atlanta
99.	"From Soweto, South Africa to Forsyth County, Georgia" Forum	28 Feb.	Atlanta
100.	"My Soul Has Been Purified" (film of Life of Winne Mandela)	22 Feb.	Atlanta
101.	"International Day for Elimination of Racial Discrimination" Woodruff Library – Mayor Young, GCDSA, SAPEP	21 March	Atlanta
102.	"Witness to Apartheid" – Downtown Branch of AFPL	9 April	Atlanta
103.	Africa Peace Tour (APT) – IBEW Auditorium	15 April	Atlanta
104.	APT "Black Women, Health and Liberation" Spelman College, Spelman College Women's Center	15 April	Atlanta
105.	Black Single Parents' Support Group		
106.	AFT Africa's Problem and U.S. Foreign Policy	15 April	Atlanta
107.	Mandela Film – South Africa Views of Apartheid	30 April	Atlanta
108.	South Africa Youth Day Rally – March to Coke HQ	16 June	Atlanta
109.	Talk Show with Julian Bond and David Ndaba on cultural boycott and Paul Simon Concert	Sept.	Atlanta
110.	Franklin Methodist Church	Oct.	Franklin, NC
111.	SCLC Women	Oct.	Atlanta, GA
112.	Interdenominational Theological Center	Oct.	Atlanta
113.	Friendship Baptist Church	Oct.	Atlanta
114.	Emory University	Oct.	Atlanta
115.	Agnes Scott College	Oct.	Atlanta
116.	Events to publicize the Fall 1988 tour of AMANDLA	Oct.	Atlanta
117.	Information Specialist for the Zimbabwe Embassy – potluck	Oct.	Atlanta
118.	Danile Landignwe – South African speaker imprisoned on Robben Island press talk at Concerned Black Clergy	Oct.	Atlanta

1988

January-March 1988 Quarterly Report

119.	Educational speaking tour pre-election	Jan. 20-24	Iowa
120.	Hunger Awareness program	Jan. 29-31.	Asheville, NC
121.	Radio interview: WAOK, WRFG		Atlanta, GA
122.	*Night Watch* with Charlie Rose & guest, Dennis Goldberg	Feb. 2	Washington, DC
123.	*Frontline,* PBS panel discussion – series on South Africa national TV		
124.	Wheeler High School		Marietta, GA
125.	Catholic Church		Macon, GA
126.	St. Phillips, AME church		Decatur, GA
127.	Christian Council with Missionaries from Kansas who worked in SA		Atlanta, GA

128.	Southern Africa Awareness Week (2nd)
	    Discussions, films, public schools
	    Friendship Baptist Church Sunday School
		Feb. 14-20	Atlanta

Oglethorpe Elementary
Southside High School
Sister Claire Muhammad School
Moslem Elementary
Georgia State University
Atlanta Junior College
International Theological Center
Morehouse College
Concerned Black Clergy meeting at Pascals
American Federation of State, County, and Municipal Employees
Gate City Heritage House
Public Library
Christ the King Cathedral
St. Peter and Paul Catholic Church

1988   *minutes*

129.	Candlelight vigil protesting impending execution of the Sharpeville Six with ITC, Amnesty International, Concerned Black Clergy, other peace/justice groups	21 March	Atlanta
130.	Student Coalition Against Apartheid and Racism workshops	25-26 March	Atlanta
131.	Reception for Asheke, Namibian Representative to the UN	27 March	Atlanta
132.	"Myth, Reality, and the Future in Southern Africa" Carter Center		Atlanta
133.	Africa Peace Tour – Southwest USA - Texas, New Mexico, Arizona	18-25 April	
134.	National Alliance of Third World Journalists conference. President Sam Nujoma keynote – AFSC co-hosts reception	April 24	Atlanta SWAPO
135.	Disarmament/ Peace and Justice Women's Group Rally.		Cape Canaveral, FL
136.	Grinnell College		Iowa
137.	Albany State College		Albany, GA
138.	Prairieview A&M University		Texas
139.	Wheeler H.S.		Marietta, GA
140.	Marist H.S.		Ashford-Dunwoody, GA
141.	Conyers Middle School		Conyers, GA
142.	Morrow H.S.		Morrow, GA
143.	Lassiter H.S.		North Marietta, GA
144.	Interdenominational Theological Center "From Luthuli to Mandela: The Struggle Goes on" - 1st Pan African Christian Conference	July 18	Atlanta, GA

Fall 1988 Quarterly Report

145.	Black Catholic Women's Conference workshops	Oct.1	Atlanta
146.	MLK, Jr. Center – Mahatma Gandhi Birthday Celebration	Oct. 1	Atlanta
147.	Disciplined Order of Christ events -church and community	Oct. 7-9	Nashville, TN

148.	Young Democrats, Georgia State University	Oct. 12	Atlanta
149.	North Cobb High School Oct. 13Atlanta		
150.	Women in the Civil Rights Movement Conference	Oct. 14-14	Atlanta MLK Center
151.	Peachtree Christian Church	Oct. 19	Atlanta
152.	Phillip's Academy	Oct. 21-22	Andover, MA
153.	United Methodist Women - several engagements	Oct. 23	Franklin, NC
154.	South Gwinnett High School	Oct. 25	Snellville, GA
155.	Interdenominational Theological Center with ministers	Oct. 27	Atlanta, GA
156.	International Day Fair – keynote	Oct. 27	Atlanta
157.	Georgia State University, English Creative Writing	Oct. 31	Atlanta
158.	African Student Union	Nov. 6	Athens
159.	Carter Center Workshop with Dr. Dudley Week	Nov. 11	Atlanta
160.	United Methodist Church	Nov. 16	Decatur, GA

1989

Winter 1989 Quarterly Report

161.	Black History Month – annual week of Awareness on Southern Africa.		
162.	Alabama Youth for Peace and Justice	14 Jan.	
163.	Gwinnett Presbyterian Family Supper	15 Jan.	
164.	Kuumba Cultural Group	16-17 Jan.	Houston, TX
165.	Coalition for Health in Southern Africa (CHISA)	19 Jan.	Atlanta, GA
166.	Emory University "Cry Freedom" film panel discussion	20 Jan.	Atlanta
167.	St. Andrews Presbyterian Church	22 Jan.	Atlanta
168.	South Gwinnett High School – 5 lectures	25 Jan.	Atlanta
169.	TV Channel- 8 taped programs		
170.	Warren United Methodist Church	26 Jan.	Atlanta
171.	Holy Innocent Episcopal Church	29 Jan.	Sandy Springs, GA
172.	Edwards High School	30 Jan.	Rockdale County
173.	Women's Association, Saddlebrook Subdivision	31 Jan.	Kennesaw, GA
174.	CHISA – health issues and Farmers Market	3 Feb.	
175.	AME Flipper Temple Church	4 Feb.	
176.	Brownson Presbyterian Church	5 Feb.	Pine Hill, NC
177.	AFSC Kansas City, MO schools, churches, colleges, radio, and television stations, press interviews	6-8 Feb.	Kansas City,
178.	Tsietsi Maleho – Release Nelson Mandela Committee. Thandi organizing and accompanying to talks and interviews	9-12 Feb.	Atlanta, GA
179.	St. Phillips AME Church Conference	11 Feb.	Columbia, SC
180.	Georgia State University graduate class	13 Feb.	
181.	Western North Carolina University	16 Feb.	Cullowhee, NC
182.	Spelman College – Mrs. Grasa Machel Visit	20 Feb.	Atlanta, GA
183.	St. Marks United Methodist Church	22 Feb.	Atlanta
184.	Amnesty International Death Penalty Campaign	24-25 Feb.	Nashville, TN
185.	West Hills Presbyterian Church	26 Feb.	Atlanta, GA
186.	Amnesty International (news article)	March	Charleston, SC

Spring 1989 Quarterly Report

187.	National Conference of Independent Schools	March	Boston, MA
188.	Unitarian Universalist Service Committee training session	March	Waveland, MI
189.	Glen Memorial Chapel at Emory University	March	Atlanta, GA
190.	St. Andrews Presbyterian Church		Tucker, GA
191.	Amnesty International, College of Charleston		Charleston, SC
192.	Morehouse College		Atlanta, GA
193.	Georgia College		Milledgeville, GA
194.	Lassiter High School		Atlanta, GA
195.	Therrell High School		Atlanta
196.	Open Door Community		Atlanta
197.	Texaco Oil Company annual shareholders meeting	9 May	Atlanta

Summer 1989 Minutes SERO Exec 8-89

198.	Concerned Black Clergy	June 12	Atlanta, GA
199.	Clark Communication Center	June 13-15	Atlanta Clark,
	Morehouse, Spelman Colleges incoming students	June 14	Atlanta
200.	"Working to End Apartheid" Conference and workshops	June 24	Atlanta
201.	Mrs. Albertina Sisulu Delegation	July 4	Atlanta
202.	Weekly presentations at 5 YMCA camps	July – Aug	Atlanta
203.	Governor's Honors Program for students	July 12	Charleston, SC
204.	Christian Youth Summer Camp	July 20	Selma, AL
205.	Rally Against Apartheid/South African Women's Day	Aug. 9	Atlanta, GA

Thandi visiting South Africa beginning August 10th. Soter lrusota covers program events and multiple speaking engagements.

Fall 1989 – Quarterly Report

206. Amnesty International Human Rights Fair	Oct. 28 S	Sandersville, GA
207. Friends Meeting	Nov. 14	Athens, GA
208. Kennesaw College	Nov. 22	Kennesaw, GA

1990 - 1996 AFSC REPORTS BECOME LESS DETAILED

209.	Quarterly Reports reflect increase in speaking engagement requests upon release of Nelson Mandela. Thandi travels to Namibia and South Africa. Helps host visit of Nelson and Winne Mandela to Atlanta	June 27, 1990	
210.	Nelson Mandela International Reception Committee	6 June	Atlanta, GA

1991

January 4, 1991 - Program Report & February 1991 Program Quarterly Report

211.	3 churches, 2 high schools,	Dec. 1990/Jan & Feb. 1991	Atlanta, GA
212.	International Theological Center (ITC)		
213.	Subcommittee of the Gate City Bar"		

Appendix C: Thandi Gcabashe Speaking Engagements 197

214.	Parker School		Chicago, IL

AFSC Anti-Apartheid newsletter Summer 1991

215.	St. Louis Community College Coke Committee	April	Forest Park, IL

May 1991 Program Quarterly Report

216. Talks at schools, communities, and organizations in South Carolina, North Carolina, Alabama, parts of Georgia, and Kansas City, MO to promote Coke Boycott.

1992

Winter, Dec-Feb 91/92 Quarterly Report

217.	ANC Deputy President Walter Sisulu's visit	Atlanta, GA
218.	Amherst College Amherst, MA	
219.	Bishop Desmond Tutu Reception for community activists	Atlanta
220.	Black History Month	
221.	Commemoration of SOWETO	Montgomery, AL
222.	Coalition for Health in South Africa (CHISA) meeting	New York City
223.	Wesleyan Nursing Home	Atlanta, GA

June-August Quarterly Report

224.	Staff speaking engagements Atlanta, Montgomery,	New York, Washington, DC

Thandi travels to South Africa with AFSC Violence Fact Finding Team.

225. Atlanta media tour for Violence Fact Finding Team

September-November Quarterly Report

226. Atlantans for Democracy in South Africa

1993

227.	Stations of the Cross – Clergy & Laity Concerned (CALC)	Atlanta, GA
228.	Friendship Force – orientation of forty-one-person group to visit South Africa	Atlanta

1994

229.	Minority Student Affairs, University of Miami Student Conference	Feb.	Coral Gables, FL
230.	Women for International Peace and Arbitration	March	Los Angeles, CA

March-June – Quarterly Report

Thandi travels with delegation to observe 1994
South Africa elections and to vote.

231.	"1994 Elections in South Africa"	May	Atlanta, GA

Summer June-August – Quarterly Report

232.	USIA conference on South Africa	Atlanta, GA
233.	Africa Cultural Olympiad – myriad of events for Thandi	
234.	Atlanta Project	
235.	National Assembly for Laity and Clergy Concerned	
236.	Fellowship of Reconciliation	
237.	two speaking engagements with two T.V. stations	

September-December – Quarterly Report

238.	University of North Carolina at Charlotte (UNCC)	Charlotte, NC
239.	John C. Smith	Charlotte
240.	Georgia State	Atlanta, GA
241.	Chapman in California	Orange, CA
242.	California Institute of Technology	Pasadena, CA

Topics ranged from: "Analysis of South Africa's Elections,"
"Challenges Facing the New South Africa,"
"Prospects for Prosperity in South Africa: social/political/economic,"
to "Future of Democracy in South Africa."

Appendix D

Reflections and observations on my visit to South Africa

From: Tandi Gcabashe
Subject: Reflections and observations on my visit to South Africa
Date: October 26, 1989

After nearly 19 years away from South Arica, my return home was filled with profound elation at seeing my family and friends once again. The entire feeling was, however, tinged with anxiety and concern that after all these years, South Africa remains a land where more than 80 percent of its people are non-persons by law.

I was, however, most impressed with the resilience of the people and the overwhelming dedication of the youth who had long since forsaken personal comforts and security, to sacrifice daily for freedom and the liberation of their country.

It was in this frame of mind that I observed my six-week stay.

People's spirit of Defiance:

July 1989: Black South Africans were generally determined to defy the heinous apartheid laws. Unbanning organizations, ignoring individual restrictions, holding meetings without permits, demanding treatment at whites-only hospitals and desegregating schools and beaches.

New Phase of Struggle: Politics of Negotiation

We are nowhere near negotiations yet, but discussions, debates, promises and proposals are beginning to focus on negotiations! The Organization of African Unity (OAU), Mass Democratic Movement (MDM), ANC, UN Special Committee, the Frontline States, and the South African Democratic Party are all taking about negotiations. Even the National Party mentioned the word negotiations 14 times in its 5-year plan!

September 6th Presidential Campaign:

The prevailing thought amongst us Africans is that the 1989 elections were the last within the fringes of the political process.

The Nationalist Party campaigned on the theme of ending the international isolation and the subsequent suffering economy.

I was amazed at how the ailing economy was commonly and openly discussed in the print as well as the electronic media. The U.S. 1986 Congressional sanctions legislation is blamed for the economic woes.

State of the economy:

Unemployment runs at 45 percent. The inflation rate is 14 percent. It must be noted, however, that inflation and unemployment are note caused by sanctions, they have been part of the South African economy since 1970. The situation is thought to be the consequence of mechanization and the general downturn in the economy. Low annual growth rate and low profits have prompted "disinvestment" more than legislation and moral persuasion. In other words, the multinational firms that are jumping on the divestment bandwagon, and are "pulling out of South Africa," in the main, are not doing so for their abhorrence of the evil of apartheid. Rather, the current low profit margins or their South African holdings have prompted their moves.

General Sales Tax (GST) has sky-rocketed to 13 percent. CONTRARY TO OUR OPPONENTS' ASSERTIONS, SANCTIONS WORK. Stronger, punitive, more comprehensive sanctions are needed to raise the price of apartheid. Raise the "premium" to apartheid's international trade.

The assessment of the political scene by the MDM leadership in South Africa is that:

- The racist government is in the worst political and economic crisis. Masses of the oppressed have rendered themselves ungovernable through actions such as the Defiance Campaign.
- The minority government has lost control and has its back to the wall.
- The government is searching for a way to relieve the pressure.
- Repression has not worked.
- Promised of so-called reforms have heretofore not worked.

Therefore, the government is desperately looking for a way out by talking about negotiations.

The pressure tactics of sanctions internationally, and the internal resistance to the evil laws of apartheid, have worked. The combination of these tactics has brought us this far. Rather than slacken the pressure, we need to accelerate it until apartheid is abolished.

Appendix D: Reflections and observations on my visit to South Africa

The Need to Understand Motive Behind Talk of Negotiations. Why Now?

- Has the government of South Africa and its white constituency undergone moral conversion?
- After years of arrogant domination and selfishness, has there been a sudden repentance and willingness to mend its ways? I think not!

Rather, the political and economic pressure exerted on the regime over the years, has taken its toll. Negotiation talk is a pragmatic political decision in the face of mounting pressure. President F. W. de Klerk's track record does not suggest that he is more liberal than his predecessors.

Since 1960, after the Sharpeville massacre, when the African National Congress took the case of South Africa to the United Nations and requested sanctions, the rationale behind sanctions has been:

- Sanctions are the last means of peaceful solution to the problem.
- Sanctions would hasten the end to the suffering rather than prolong it.
- Sanctions would avert a blood-bath.
- Sanctions would bring all parties to the negotiation table.
- ANC has always seen negotiations as the final stage in the struggle for a nonracial democratic South Africa.

Preconditions to negotiations should be seen as a necessary and reasonable demand. A climate conducive to talks, a climate of free political activity must exist before free and fair negotiations occur.

The DEMANDS are:

1. Release of all political prisoners and detainees.
2. Unban organizations and lift restrictions on individuals.
3. Lift the State of Emergency and security legislation.
4. Repeal apartheid laws.
5. Remove troops from the Townships.
6. Return of exiles without let or hinderance.

WORD OF CAUTION TO ANTI-APARTHEID ACTIVISTS.

Our collective labors and sacrifices of the past have ushered in a new phase of the struggle – the Phase of Negotiations.

We must be vigilant. We must not be coerced into accepting empty promises and half-step measures. In our anxiety to see a return to peace and freedom in South

Africa, we might be tempted to accept anything that looks like an olive branch. Remember, the enemy is cunning and old in the game of double talk and duplicity.

APPENDIX E

"1994 Elections in South Africa"
Presented by Thandi Gcabashe
Speech Delivered at the Quaker Meeting House
Decatur, Georgia, May 1994

Upon Thandi's return from election observations in South Africa
(Transcription by Heather Gray)

Friends, Sisters and Brothers:

On this grand occasion on a beautiful evening in Atlanta celebrate and rejoice the triumph of justice, peace, freedom, and equality over injustice, violence, and inequality that characterized South Africa for many decades. We have witnessed an end of an era in history. A powerful moment in history, marking the end of apartheid. We have witnessed a people who had the will to, first of all, survive the pain and suffering of apartheid for many years and who demonstrated the same strong will against odds at election.

Due to this struggle many of us have had to flee South Africa. I'm a South African as you know. And I've been in exile for 24 years. I was one of many, many who returned to South Africa to vote for the first time in my country. But I know also that many fellow South Africans present in this room, who could not make the journey, who voted in absentia. You, too, were counted in what constituted the freedom in our country. I want to take this opportunity, though, to acknowledge the Atlanta community and, in particular, the American Friends Service Committee, and the Atlanta Friends Meeting, the Quaker Meeting, for the support they have rendered me over the years.

I would like to ask all those who traveled to South Africa in our group to please rise and be recognized wherever you are in the room. You see here an indomitable group with courage and spirit. Efforts were made by those opposed to democracy to intimidate the international community by increased acts of violence close to the election time. This group said, "No, we shall not be cowed." In addition to the courage, the energy and determination of this group that went into determining the financial aspects of this trip is admired and appreciated.

As we left Atlanta for South Africa last month, we knew we were about to witness history in the making. Not that we didn't have some fears and underlying speculation of the possible dangers ahead, it's that all of us were fortunate enough to represent the Atlanta community in the South African elections and were acutely aware that we were about to take part in events that would end an era and give birth to a new nation. That was great!

What role were we to play in the electoral process? The African National Congress had requested that the international community be present during the elections. Though the international election observers for the elections from the United States, of which there were approximately 200, were in South Africa under the auspices of the Lawyers Committee for Civil Rights Under the Law from Washington DC, there were international observers as well from the United Nations, the Organization of African Unity, the European Community Union, and the Commonwealth. In addition to instructing/guiding the US observers, the Lawyers Committee also assisted the South Africa Independent Electoral Commission, or the IEC, in the overall observing and monitoring of the election. There were eleven South African members appointed to serve on the IEC and five international appointments. Gay McDougall of the Lawyers Committee was one of the five international members appointed to the IEC. The others were from Canada, Zimbabwe, Eritrea, and Sweden.

As observers, our task was two-fold. Specifically, we were asked to provide a clear international presence during the electoral process; to also observe the electoral process as it took place with a view to the extent to which it was free and fair. Angela King, who is the chief of the United Nations Observer Mission in South Africa, described the international presence as being, and I quote her, "To achieve, an environment in South Africa free from violence, coercion, and intimidation or fear, thus allowing the overwhelming majority population of the country to cast their vote with confidence and enthusiasm to determine their own destiny and to unite and educate themselves to build a new South Africa."

When we arrived in South Africa we were impressed with the IEC and the Lawyers Committee training. The professionalism of the three-day training set the tone for our election observing.

Following the training our Atlanta group was deployed to three separate areas. We went to the provinces of Natal - and I was one of the people who went to Natal, and some of you may know that this is my home province so I was at home there. Also, you will remember that KwaZulu Natal is the province that was the one plagued with violence most of all.

So, we were deployed to the provinces of Natal, Eastern Cape, Transvaal, and the Western Cape, which is Cape Town.

I am always very, very jealous when I mention the name Cape Town because of the kind of war going on between Durban and Cape Town as to which city is the most beautiful. Ummm - I think Durban is!

What impressed all of us about the elections…what is it that we got from the elections…? is that people came out in droves to the polling stations in a way that the IEC could not have anticipated. In fact, it was discovered, somehow shamefully, that the South African government population statistics were far understated. They were understating the black population. Oh, there could be many reasons for that. Our births were not registered accurately, the deaths, as well and a myriad of other reasons.

What else impressed us during those days of elections? There were those long lines in the rain, in the hot sun, from dawn to dusk. Often people waiting in line without food or water. And yet, people waited patiently and tenaciously to make their mark on the ballot. That mark was so important to those South Africans who waited in those long lines. It was the mark of their lives. In some instances, people returned on the second and third day before they could vote.

There were several reasons for this. The IEC, of course, was charged with organizing, supervising, and then finally declaring it free and fair and as well as adjudicating in cases of disputes. Four months was not long enough to organize this efficiently, especially for a country were 84% of the population had not participated in elections before. Also, a country where 60% of that 84% is illiterate.

And I'm always very quick to point out that just because people are illiterate does not mean they are ignorant. They knew exactly where to put that "X" mark.

The patience and the tenacity were amazing. A lot of the people had expected - they had waited - all their lives for this day and a few more hours or days in line are worth it. They came from far and wide - some in wheelbarrows, others on stretchers, some were walking on canes, and some on buses and trains and so forth. Some had their children on their backs.

One elderly woman said this to me, "I'm not casting this vote for myself anymore, but for my grandchildren." This is a woman who suffered and struggled for years and was casting a vote for her grandchildren.

My own mother, of course, who is 90 years old, voted as well from a wheelchair. I had hoped I would cast my vote with my mother, but there was some confusion about the polling station where she was to vote, so I missed that opportunity, but the most important thing is that she voted and I voted as well.

My father once said, "There remains before us the building of a new land, a home for all who are black, white, and brown, from the ruins of the old narrow groups, a synthesis of the rich cultural strains, which we have inherited." We saw the beginnings of that in the voting line, which was a culture unto itself. People who had never before communicated reached across racial lines, chatted; they shared experiences; they even shared cold drinks. I saw a few times when that happened, while in line. This was a miracle. As Bishop Tutu said, "A miracle descended upon our nation on those three days."

What was most impressive about the election, though, in addition to the long lines, was the involvement of the South Africans in every step of the way from voter education to the campaigning, to the voting and to the counting of the vote. People were brought close to the process. They now have ownership in the intricate processes of democracy. You really felt that people had a feel for these elections in their hearts and minds. At the voting centers as well as in the counting centers, South Africans were presiding officers. They were voting staff, they were with peace monitors, they were enumerators counting the votes, they were observers, they were party agents, they were voting citizens. It all happened at once.

The counting of the votes: I must mention the counting of the ballots because it was fascinating. I am sure my colleagues who were in South Africa with me would bear me out on this one. The painstaking process first of the reconciling of the ballots. There had to be a balance between the ballots that were sent to the voting station and the ballots that were returned to the counting centers.

The unfilling of the ballot boxes often generated great discussion and debate. There was not always agreement about whether or not the boxes had been tampered with. There were some wild stories concerning that. I know because I was in KwaZulu and I was out in the rural, remote areas of KwaZulu in a place called uMkhanyakude, and my other partners in the group with me were also in a place called uMgungundlovu - nice names – uMkhanyakude, uMgungundlovu. Often when we were driving at night through the bushes, we expected to see people carrying ballot boxes on their head. Anyhow, but that's part of the democracy that arrived to our people of South Africa.

The counting of the votes - it was amazing. After the ballot boxes were opened and there was agreement that they had not been tampered with, the contents are emptied and then counted. They were held up in full few of everybody - observers, monitors, party agents, so that all of us could see on the ballot the party that had been X marked. Now, remember (they said) there were more than 23 million people voting in South Africa and they voted on a provincial as well as a national ballot. That meant that … each one of those ballots was held up to full view until there was agreement that the ballot was valid and to which party it belonged.

The inauguration was the culminating event at the Union Buildings in Pretoria when Nelson Mandela the Prisoner became Nelson Mandela the President of South Africa.

Really, that was the moment of moments. Most of those of you who are in the room know the campaign for the release of Mandela started as though it could never be achieved. But we persisted. We went around with those petitions everywhere in Atlanta - everywhere in the nation - asking people to sign onto the petition that Nelson Mandela and all of the political prisoners should be released.

Most of those people who were released from Robben Island are now holding office in the new government of national unity in South Africa. I was amazed when the results of the election were announced. South Africa is now divided into nine regions instead of the previous four regions. And out of the nine regions, seven of the premiers, or governors, are ANC ex-prisoners, or ex-UDF (United Democratic Front) members. But the eighth premier is Gatsha Buthelezi. I'm really never going to tell how Gatsha Buthelezi won Natal. And you (ask) why I'm not going to tell it's because at the end of the election the IEC - the Independent Electoral Commission - made an announcement that election had been substantially fair and free.

The festivities, the exhilaration as people spontaneously danced, kissed, and surely transformed Pretoria into a people's government building. No one had ever seen that previously in Pretoria.

This was my first attendance at an inaugural ceremony, but it was wonderful. There were 180 heads of state and just watching them coming in with their different contingencies - it was beautiful.

I had been to Pretoria before to make arrangement for my mother - as I said, she was 90 years old - just to understand the landscape and the logistics about getting her to where she needed to go for the inauguration.

And the inaugural committee, I asked them, I said, "You have a most difficult task making arrangement for these 180 heads of state." And they said, "Yeah." And I said to them, "And you've never done this before? I hope you can enlist the help of the previous government because they have experienced doing this kind of thing." And you know the answer I was given? "No, they don't have any kind of experience." "Why?" "Because South Africa never had any international visitors at their inaugural celebration." So it was everybody's first experience.

There were 6,000 VIPs at the amphitheater and some 50,000 people in the lawn below. There's a picture somewhere of the South African Union Building. And it is truly beautiful, constructed on a hill right at the top of Pretoria, and then the beautiful garden descending down to the city below.

I had never been to the Union Building, of course, to the building itself. But I've been to the grounds of the building. In 1956 when we were protesting the passbook, we were 20,000 strong black women and we were allowed onto the rise at the bottom of the hill and then from there we sent our petition to the president telling him that we would never carry the passbook. But now I was celebrating. I was one of the 6,000 VIPs.

The expression "many cultures, one nation" is the one that you will hear a lot mentioned in South Africa. And this was truly expressed in the variation of the cultural diets on the menu at the elaborate luncheon that we attended after the ceremony. Examples of how diverse this luncheon was - the menu ... (text missing). There was also an Afrikaner dish. And other western style food, of course.

The luncheon was so elaborate, it was so festive that the thought that crossed my mind, "Well, Nelson, you have introduced this new South Africa, with a bang. You've really done this so well. Now we're going to hold you to this standard."

I attended this with my 90-year-old mother, of course, who said at one point to me, "I will be the first to tell the story to you father when I depart." And that is my father who would be 97 years old had he not been assassinated.

Now, the celebrations are over. Nelson Mandela is the president of South Africa. Let's start the business of building South Africa. And before I get to that let me just mention that while the VIPs and thousands of South Africans celebrated in Pretoria, the entire country was in a state of ecstasy and celebration. The Soweto streets were alive with tables, with food, with drinks, with flowers, with balloons - and people were dancing and undulating - chanting - truly enjoying the grandeur of the moment.

The message from Nelson Mandela repeatedly was to forgive and forget. His was not simply a message, but Mandela's demeanor and persona is the embodiment of the spirit of reconciliation. There's no bitterness in the man. There's no rancour. There's no revengefulness. Mandela is the epitome of what he's asking the country to do. And I hope that all of us South Africans abroad and in South Africa will heed him.

Now we are faced with the tremendous task of restoring the beauty and glory of our country in a nonracial, democratic, and unitary South Africa. Reconstruction is at hand. It will be as formidable and challenging, if not more, than the task of ending apartheid.

Poverty is the single greatest burden of South Africa's people - a direct result of the apartheid system. Poverty effects millions of people, the majority of whom live in rural areas and are women.

The priority areas designated by the African National Congress are in the Reconstruction and Development Program to address the devastation of apartheid. These include job creation through public works programs and the provision of basic needs such as land reform, housing and services, water and sanitation, energy and electrification, telecommunication, transport, environment, nutrition, healthcare, social security, and social welfare.

What a tall order!

Programs of reconstruction, development, and reconciliation: South Africans call upon your support and assistance in implementing these programs. President Clinton appears to be well disposed and sympathetic toward the new South Africa. He has pledged $600 million over a period of three years, but he could be encouraged to do more. Some of you will remember that after the devastation of Europe after WWII what was needed was a real very, very serious plan of rebuilding Europe - the Marshall Plan. South Africa needs a plan of that kind, even if the World Bank and the International Monetary Fund come with strings attached and in the long term are not in the interest of developing countries. To Clinton's credit he has encouraged other western countries to make similar overtures toward South Africa.

The time is now to wear another hat - a development hat, and a reconstruction hat. The transition will be difficult. The people's expectations are high and unless they are reasonably met, this young democracy will crumble.

America is South Africa's number one trading partner after Britain. As sanctions have been lifted the international business community is once again beginning to invest in our country under a code of conduct developed by the South African unions, the South African Council of Churches, and business in South Africa, as well as input from the US anti-apartheid movement. The role of non-governmental organizations also has to be part of the reconstruction phase. That includes you who are here tonight. Your help and assistance are needed in what the Americans Friends Service Committee refers to as people-to-people conduct.

The AFSC was instrumental in developing a sister city relationship with Braklaagte in Bophuthatswana - between Braklaagte and Atlanta - to encourage church-to-church, school-to-school, farmer-to-farmer relationships. At the moment the Atlanta-Braklaagte Project is seeking funding or donations for a tractor for the people of Braklaagte.

Finally, let me deal with an issue that is very important in the long run. Finally, what does a free South Africa symbolize? It is good to celebrate. It is good to eat and be merry. But seriously what does this vote mean for South Africa?

In 1992, the UN Secretary General said of the transition, "It was of historic proportions what was about to take place in South Africa," and that's exactly what we observed when we were there. In South Africa we have witnessed an historical and unique and dramatic change of one type of government to another, which is referred to as the relatively peaceful and dramatic change from the apartheid government of the National Party to the government of national unity controlled by those who were oppressed under apartheid.

It's very rare in the history of man that such a change of power would occur without bloodshed. And this is unique about the South African election.

I need to say that I am not here to promote President de Klerk because he was raised Afrikaner from cradle up to the age that he is today. He was also in Parliament for 17 years. There was a time that he also held portfolio of the Minister of Education, education that has devastated the youth of South Africa. Some call it the "Lost Generation" today.

But, this peaceful transition would not have occurred without his consent. He, in a way, conceded power. And I'm not saying "willingly." There were probably a whole lot of circumstances that caused him to do so. He could have simply buried his head in the sand and dragged the whole nation into a bloody war. But he did not do that.

A free South Africa also means an end of isolation, in that South Africa has been readmitted into the family of nations. It means not only the end of the worst form of racism in our century, but most significantly, the end of colonialism in Africa.

It means an end to the destabilization, the devastation, and the poverty forced upon the people of southern Africa—as in Namibia, Angola, Mozambique, Zambia, and others—who have been dominated by the South African apartheid system for too long. It means that the world will stop referring to South Africa in negative terms such as "the evil, the wicked system, the immoral, the repugnant,"—and the one that I didn't say, that de Klerk hated the most, "the regime."

This change in Africa also symbolizes the ushering in of a new nation with the prospects of peace and recovery for many millions of people in the region, and has the potential of exacting a positive influence on African affairs, because much of Africa has been marginalized for too long. And, with the assistance of the international community and the success of democracy in South Africa, it might help pull Africa out of its political and economic quagmire.

As a South African, thank you for your support all these many years. I look forward to seeing you in the next South African election in 1999.

Thank you.

Appendix F
Sampling of Newspaper Articles – 1981 - 1994

Note: Articles from *The Atlanta Journal, The Atlanta Constitution,* and *The Atlanta Journal Constitution* are written as *Atlanta Journal Constitution*. Page numbers are as in print.

1981
Horn, Elaine. "Daughter Follows in Nobel Prize-Winning Father's Footsteps." *Atlanta Journal Constitution*. October 22, 1981. Page D-9.

Sack, Kevin. "Exiles struggle for change in South Africa." *Atlanta Journal Constitution*. November 8, 1981. Page 34-A.

Bailey, Sharon. "Woman's work against apartheid motivated by personal memories." *Atlanta Journal Constitution*. November 8, 1981. Page 34-A.

1982
Barnes, Beverly D. "Atlantans Protest Policies in Southern Africa." *Atlanta Journal Constitution*. April 1, 1982. Page 10D.

Laker, Barbara. "Atlanta's women's panel hears international stories." *Atlanta Journal Constitution*. December 2, 1982. Page D-13.

1983
Yearly, Midge. "Anti-Apartheid groups spurn jazz concert." *Atlanta Journal Constitution*. April 1, 1983. Page 15-C.

AP. "U.N. chastises artists for performing in South Africa." *Atlanta Journal Constitution*. October 27, 1983. Page 23-A.

Turner, Renee D. "Memory of apartheid spurs woman on." *Atlanta Journal Constitution*. December 27, 1983. Page 10-A.

1984
"Social action: Quakers light way to peace." *Atlanta Journal Constitution*. September 8, 1984. Page 6B.

Sack, Kevin. "Exiles." *Atlanta Journal Constitution*. November 4, 1984. Pages 10,11,12,13.

Smith, Helen C. "Classic juxtapositions offer an unlikely mix for Sunday afternoon." *Atlanta Journal Constitution*. November 4, 1984. Page 2-J.

"Noble winner's daughter votes." *South Florida Sun-Sentinel*. November 7, 1984. Page 21A.

1985
"Anti-Apartheid Rally at Coca-Cola Headquarters. *The Atlanta Voice*. April 6-12, 1985.

"Councilman Lewis arrested." *Atlanta Journal Constitution*. April 30, 1985. Page 1.

White, Gayle. "Lawmakers Lewis, Brooks arrested at demonstration." *Atlanta Journal Constitution*. April 30, 1985. 12-A

"Judge dismisses charges against Brooks, Lewis." *Atlanta Journal Constitution*. May 1, 1985. Page 9.

Teepen, Tom. "Mandela still haunts Pretoria." *Atlanta Journal Constitution*. August 24, 1985. Page 14-A.

"Daughters of Nobel Prize winners lead vigil." *Atlanta Journal Constitution*. August 28, 1985. Page 1 & 4-A.

"South Africa divestiture bill introduced for fourth time." *Atlanta Journal Constitution*. August 28, 1985. Page 1.

Turner, Renee D. "2,000 attend anti-apartheid vigil at Morehouse College." *Atlanta Journal Constitution*. August 28, 1985. Page 3-A.

AP. "Tutu's Daughter Speaks At Atlanta Demonstration." *Enquirer* (Columbus, GA). August 29, 1985. Page B-5.

Hanif, C.B. "Apartheid Vigil Draws Nobel Prize Daughter." *The Atlanta Voice*. August 31st-September 6, 1985. Page 17.

"Eight who care leading the battle." *Atlanta Journal Constitution*. September 29, 1985. Page 44-A.

"Atlanta's rebel with a cause." Atlanta Journal Constitution. October 24, 1985. Page 1-C & 2-C.

"Anti-apartheid battle reaches state capitol." *Atlanta Journal Constitution*. October 24, 1985. Page 49.

"Reports from Nairobi." *Atlanta Journal Constitution*. October 26, 1985. Page 48. Huffman, Alan. "Mrs. Tutu: U.S. should back anti-apartheid efforts more." *The Clarion-Ledger/Jackson Daily News*. November 10, 1985. Page 3B.

1986
Silence, Michael. "Racism 'legal' in S. Africa, exile says." *The Knoxville News-Sentinel*. January 25, 1986. Page A8.

Lewis, Dwight. "Divestiture linked to end to apartheid." *The Tennessean*. March 30, 1986. Page 14-A.

UPI. "Vanderbilt group erects huts to protest S. African policy." *Kingsport Times-News*. March 31, 1986. Page 9A.

Pousner, Howard. "Divestment issue debated at Spelman." *Atlanta Journal Constitution*. April 26, 1986. Pages 1-B and 3-B.

Teepen, Tom. "Divesting ourselves of racism." *Atlanta Journal Constitution*. April 29, 1986. Page 8-A.

Green, Connie. "SCLC worked behind scenes to convince Coke to divest." *Atlanta Journal Constitution*. September 18, 1986. Page 17.

"Coke's sale of South Africa bottler a 'sham' protesters say." *Atlanta Journal Constitution*. October 11, 1986. Page 2D.

The New York Times. "Blacks gain little as firms leave S. Africa." *Atlanta Journal Constitution*. December 31, 1986. Page 3-A.

1987
Miller, Walter W. "U.S., allies strengthen apartheid." *Atlanta Journal Constitution*. February 2, 1987. Page 29-A.

"South Africa: Views of Apartheid." *Atlanta Journal Constitution. Calendar*. April 18, 1987. Page 48.

"South Africa divestiture bill introduced for fourth time." *Atlanta Journal Constitution*. August 28, 1987. Page 2B.

"The 'Apartheid – A Special Frontline Series.'" *Atlanta Journal Constitution. Best Bets*. December 16, 1987. Page 14-C.

1988
"Black Women's Coalition of Atlanta. *Atlanta Journal Constitution. Calendar.* March 26, 1988. Page 45.

Sullivan, Michael. "S. African blacks boycott work to mark '76 uprising." *Atlanta Journal Constitution*. June 17, 1988. Page 8.

1989
Jeffers, Gromer, Jr. "Apartheid foe predicts victory." *The Kansas City Times*. February 8, 1989. B-3.

Thompson, Bill. "Everyone who is black suffers: Native South African works to help nation throw off yoke of apartheid."*The News and Courier* (Charleston, SC). March 24, 1989. Page 1-D

Jackson, Derrick Z. "Saying no to Coke – the cola that is." *The Boston Sunday Globe*. April 16, 1989. Page 79. "College bans Coke products after anti-apartheid protests." *Bennington Banner* (Massachusetts). May 3, 1989. Page 4.

Loisel, Laurie. "Evils of apartheid described." *Daily Hampshire Gazette*. December 11, 1989. Page 9.

1990
Simpson, Constance. "Struggle Entering 'New Phase.'" *The Charlotte Observer*. February 13, 1990. Page 4D.

"Everyone who is black suffers: Native South African works to help nation throw off yoke of apartheid." *The News and Courier* (Charleston, SC). March 24, 1989.

Durcanin, Cynthia, Harvey, Steve. "Coke isn't welcome on Mandela's tour." *Atlanta Journal Constitution.* June 13, 1990. Page A-1.

Saporta, Maria. "Mandela: Coke denies it's been banned from tour." *Atlanta Journal Constitution*. June 13, 1990. Page A-9, continued from Page A1.

"Mandela marketer gears up." News Services. *The Province* (Vancouver, B.C.). June 14, 1990. Page 11.

"Salute to South African Women." *Atlanta Journal Constitution. DATEBOOK.* June 24, 1990. Page L-6.

1991

"Talk to focus on South Africa." *Daily Hampshire Gazette.* October 15, 1991. Page 10.

1992

Durcanin, Cynthia. "Apartheid foes in U.S. delighted as S. African whites listen at last." *Atlanta Journal Constitution.* March 19, 1992. Page A10.

McMillar, Colleen. "Exiled South African to speak about strife in her home country." *The Macon Telegraph.* May 19, 1992. Page 3B.

Volland, Victor. "Two Warn of S. African Anarchy: Church Observers Who Toured Country Tell of 'Appalling' Violence." *St. Louis Post-Dispatch.* November 18, 1992. Page 9A.

1993

"The future that awaits a nation and a family." *Atlanta Journal Constitution.* July 9, 1993. Page A-11.

1994

Harris, Lyle V. "South Africa or bust! But how to pay?" *Atlanta Journal Constitution.* March 27, 1994. Page A20.

Eaton, Maynard & Miller, Melody. "Atlantans Monitor South African Elections." *The Atlanta Voice.* April 1923-29, 1994. Pages 1 & 12.

Harris, Lyle V. "Vote climaxes years of struggle in South Africa." *Atlanta Journal Constitution.* April 27, 1994. Page A10.

"At home in a community moved by justice." *Atlanta Journal Constitution.* July 25, 1994. Page A13.